# Tort Law in Latvia

# Tort Law in Latvia

**Jānis Kārkliņš**
**Vadim Mantrov**
**Lauris Rasnačs**

This book was originally published as a monograph in the International Encyclopaedia of Laws/Tort Law.

Founding Editor: Roger Blanpain
General Editor: Frank Hendrickx
Volume Editor: Britt Weyts

Wolters Kluwer

*Published by:*
Kluwer Law International B.V.
PO Box 316
2400 AH Alphen aan den Rijn
The Netherlands
E-mail: lrs-sales@wolterskluwer.com
Website: www.wolterskluwer.com/en/solutions/kluwerlawinternational

*Sold and distributed by:*
Wolters Kluwer Legal & Regulatory U.S.
920 Links Avenue
Landisville, PA 17538
United States of America
E-mail: customer.service@wolterskluwer.com



ISBN 978-94-035-2386-6

e-Book: ISBN 978-94-035-2716-1
web-PDF: ISBN 978-94-035-2726-0

This title is available on www.kluwerlawonline.com

# The Authors

Dr iur Janis Karklins (Jānis Kārkliņš) is a Professor of Civil Law and Head of the Civil department at the Faculty of Law of the University of Latvia. He has been regularly appointed as an expert in legal science by the Science Council of Latvia since 2008.

His main research interests are related to civil law and its relationship with special civil law branches such as law of obligations (contract law and delict (tort) law), commercial law (especially commercial contracts), and banking law.

He is the author and co-author of approximately sixty scientific publications in Latvian and English, including those indexed in the *Scopus* and/or *Web of Science* databases. He is co-author of the monograph *Problems of Contract and Tort Law in the European Union and Latvia* (2017) in Latvian, co-author of the Springer monograph *The Law of the Baltic States* (2017) as well as a co-author of the *Kluwer Law International*-published monograph *Contract Law in Latvia.*

He has delivered papers on topical civil law issues at more than thirty international and domestic scientific conferences in Latvia and other European countries. He is a regular member of organizing committees responsible for arranging international scientific conferences at the Faculty of Law, University of Latvia. He received a Latvian state award For contribution to the development of the Register of Enterprises of the Republic of Latvia in 2013. Janis Karklins has been an official expert of the Latvian Constitutional Court on civil law aspects related to human rights. He is a member of the Promotion Council of the Faculty of Law of the University of Latvia.

He has successfully supervised and/or participated in international and domestic scientific projects, Latvian state research programmes and research programmes of the European Commission. He frequently participates as an expert in discussion of draft legal acts in ministries and committees of the Latvian parliament.

He has been practising as an attorney-at-law for more than twelve years and was admitted to the Latvian Bar Association in 2007 as an attorney. He runs his own law firm, is married and has two children.

## The Authors

Dr iur Vadim Mantrov (Vadims Mantrovs) is a Docent of Civil Law and Research Fellow at the Faculty of Law of the University of Latvia; he is also the Head of the Legal Science Institute of the Faculty of Law. He has regularly been appointed as an expert in legal science by the Science Council of Latvia since 2012.

His main research interests are related to civil law and its relationship with special civil law branches such as insurance law (as well as risk regulation in general), consumer protection, intellectual property (especially in conjunction with food law and product quality protection).

He is the author and co-author of more than eighty scientific publications in Latvian, English and Russian, including those indexed in the *Scopus* and/or *Web of Science* as well as other databases. His authored monograph published by *Springer*[1] was recognized as one of the scientific achievements in Latvian science in 2015 by the Latvian Academy of Sciences. Likewise, the Latvian Academy of Sciences recognized his co-authored monograph published by *LU Academic Press*[2] as one of the scientific achievements in Latvian science in 2018. He is an author of the monograph *Insurance Law in Latvia* as well as a co-author of the monograph *Contract Law in Latvia*, both published by *Kluwer Law International*.

He has presented and delivered papers on topical civil law issues in more than thirty international and domestic scientific conferences in Latvia and other European countries as well as outside of Europe.

He has successfully supervised and/or participated in several international and domestic scientific projects, including participation in the implementation of *Justice* projects (funded by the European Commission), a Latvian state research programme, a national grant (funded by the Scientific Council of Latvia) and internal projects of the University of Latvia. Additionally, he frequently participates as an expert in discussion of draft legal acts in committees of the Latvian parliament.

Previously, he was in legal practice for more than ten years, being admitted to the Latvian Bar Association in 2005 initially as an associate attorney but since 2008 as an attorney, though he suspended membership in 2015 due to his academic work. He has been a Latvian and European trade mark agent since 2008, though he suspended activity in 2015, again due to his academic and scientific work.

1. Mantrov, V. *EU law of indications of geographical origin*. Cham: Springer, 2014.
2. Rodiņa, A., Meikališa, Ā., Strada-Rozenberga, K., Danovskis, E., Mantrovs, V. Tiesiskais ietvars: Ieskats. Secinājumi un ieteikumi. Labā prakse. Pozitīvās tendences likumdošanā un tiesībpiemērošanā [Legal framework: Insight. Conclusions and recommendations. Good practice. Positive trends in legislation and law enforcement]. Grām.: Simtam Pāri. Viedā Latvija: Valsts pētījumu programma EKOSOC-LV 'Tautsaimniecības transformācija, gudra izaugsme, pārvaldība un tiesiskais ietvars valsts un sabiedrības ilgtspējīgai attīstībai – jaunas pieejas ilgtspējīgas zināšanu sabiedrības veidošanai' [One Hundred Years. Smart Latvia: National Research Program EKOSOC-LV 'Transforming the National Economy, Smart Growth, Governance and the Legal Framework for Sustainable Development of the State and Society – New Approaches to Creating a Sustainable Knowledge Society']. Rīga: Latvijas Zinātņu akadēmija, 2018, 223–250.lpp.

Dr iur Lauris Rasnacs (Lauris Rasnačs) is a Docent in Civil Law at the Faculty of Law of the University of Latvia.

He is the author of some twenty scientific publications in English and Latvian related to civil procedure law and alternative dispute resolution, civil law and its special branches such as competition law, commercial law and intellectual property. He is co-author of the monograph *Contract Law in Latvia*, published by Kluwer Law International. He has also translated historical legal articles from German into Latvian.

He has participated in some ten international and domestic scientific conferences.

He was an expert of the Consultative Council of the Register of Enterprises of the Republic of Latvia from 2011 to 2013. He was a member of the working group established by the Latvian Chamber of Commerce and Industry for drafting the new Latvian Arbitration Law in 2012. Since 2017 he has been a member of the permanent working group on amendments to Latvian Civil Procedure Law, as well as an expert, invited by the Constitutional Court of the Republic of Latvia to provide opinion on several matters.

Since 2007 he has been an attorney-at-law, since 2011 a trade mark agent and since 2012 a European trade mark agent.

## The Authors

# Table of Contents

# List of Abbreviations

| | |
|---|---|
| Cabinet | Cabinet of Ministers of the Republic of Latvia (*Latvijas Republikas Ministru kabinets* in Latvian) |
| BGB | German Civil Code (Bürgerliches Gesetzbuch) |
| CJEU | Court of Justice of the European Union (this term also covers the previous title of the court, that is, the European Court of Justice) |
| CL[3] | Civil Law[4] of the Republic of Latvia adopted in 1937 (*Latvijas Republikas 1937.gada Civillikums* in Latvian)[5] |
| CPL | Civil Procedure Law (*Civilprocesa likums* in Latvian) |
| DCFR | Bar, C. von, Clive, E., Schulte-Nölke, H., Beale, H., Herre, J., Huet, J., Storme, M., Swann, S., Varul, P., Veneziano, A., Zoll, F. (eds). Principles, Definitions and Model Rules of European Private Law Draft Common Frame of Reference (DCFR). Available at https://www.law.kuleuven.be/personal/mstorme/european-private-law_en.pdf |

3. Note that legal acts of the Republic of Latvia as well as other countries, e.g., Germany, are referred to in this monograph (usually in footnotes) by using abbreviations of their titles recognized in legal practice.
4. Titles of official translations of Latvian legal acts use the term 'Law' instead of 'Act'. Since this monograph covers the titles of official translations of Latvian legal acts, preference is given to the former term.
5. This monograph is prepared by reference to official texts of Latvian legal acts. At the same time, when a particular legal act is cited for the first time, reference is made to its official translation into English. These are prepared by the State Language Centre on the basis of the Regulation of the State Language Centre (no official translation into English available) Point 2 of which provides that one of the Centre's aims is to ensure state administrative institutions and society have access to official translations of legal acts and other documents issued by state and international organizations. These translations are available either on the web-page of the State Language Centre (available at https://vvc.gov.lv/index.php?route=product/category&path=60_109) or on the web-page of Latvian legal acts (available at www.likumi.lv). Though these translations are prepared by a competent state institution, they are not approved by the legislator. Official translations may not be updated and might not use appropriate legal terms.

**List of Abbreviations**

| | |
|---|---|
| EC | European Community |
| EEC | European Economic Community |
| EEZ | European Economic Zone |
| EU | European Union |
| USSR | Union of Soviet Socialist Republics |
| KCL | Commercial Law (*Komerclikums* in Latvian) |
| OJ | Official Journal of the European Union |
| OECD | Organisation for Economic Co-operation and Development |
| PETL | Principles of European Tort Law |
| GDP | Gross Domestic Product |
| Supreme Court | Supreme Court of the Republic of Latvia (*Latvijas Republikas Augstākā tiesa* in Latvian), covering any department of the court; please note that it is also possible to use its alternative title, i.e., the Senate |

# Preface

This monograph deals with the regulation of tort law – the law of non-contractual civil liability – in Latvia by discussing its main concepts and institutions together with their underlying prevailing theories and topical court practice. The monograph has been prepared by a team of three recognized and experienced Latvian scholars who simultaneously are or have also been civil law practitioners. The monograph is prepared with the aim of providing an international audience with an understanding of how tort law is regulated in Latvia and of its contents in conjunction with problems identified in both Latvian legal literature and Latvian legal practice and leading opinions in terms of resolving them as expressed in Latvian legal literature or court practice. The authors would like to believe that the monograph will be a valuable, practical, and comprehensive guide to Latvian tort law for those interested in getting to know its concepts and institutes.

This monograph continues the discussion of Latvian civil law for an international audience previously commenced by the late Professor Kalvis Torgāns[6] and the present team of co-authors who jointly prepared a monograph on Latvian contract law.[7] Consequently, the present monograph addresses another part of civil law and specifically deals with tort law – the law of non-contractual civil liability.

Much of what has been said in the preface to the previous monograph is also true concerning the regulation of tort law in Latvia.

As already noted in the preface to the monograph on Latvian contract law, the fact that Latvia is a relatively small country in north-eastern Europe does not mean that its contract regulation fails to demonstrate significant legal problems and solutions to those problems.[8] The same conclusion to an even greater extent applies to tort regulation in Latvia. Tort law is largely based on national traditions, theories, and policy considerations which largely differ from one country to another. Latvia is no exception to this general rule, testifying to the necessity for the present monograph.

Tort law in Latvia is generally based on regulation included in the currently effective Civil Law, restored in 1992–1993. A few subsequent amendments to the Civil Law concern regulation of torts. However, more important developments may be found in other legal acts governing separate torts (such as product liability or torts

6. *See* his obituary in the recent issue of the Journal of University of Latvia 'Law' (Rozenfelds, J. In Memoriam. Kalvis Torgāns. Journal of University of Latvia 'Law', 2021, No 14, p. 5).
7. Torgāns, K., Kārkliņš, J., Mantrov, V., Rasnačs, L. *Contract Law in Latvia*. AH Alphen aan den Rijn: Kluwer, 2020.
8. *Ibid.*, p. 17.

in environmental law) or specific matters concerning certain torts in addition to their regulation in Part Four of the Civil Law as a part of regulation of the law of obligations (such as road traffic torts). All these aspects were considered during the preparation of this monograph.

This monograph is the first comprehensive publication in English on Latvian tort law to systematically reflect its general and specific issues. Previously, several scientific publications were published in English by Latvian legal scholars dealing with specific issues of Latvian tort law such as the concept of strict liability[9] and exceptions to imposition of strict liability in the case of source of abnormal danger,[10] compensation of non-pecuniary damage caused in road traffic accidents in the context of EU motor insurance law,[11] and other issues.[12] In addition, there are publications on Latvian tort law in general, for instance, a chapter on non-contractual obligations (i.e., torts) in Latvia in a monograph on the law of the Baltic states.[13] However, due to the character of these publications, they do not systematically and comprehensively deal with Latvian tort law as does this monograph. Therefore, an international audience – including foreign legal scholars, practitioners, policymakers and other interested persons – who are not familiar with Latvian tort law could not have a complete picture of tort regulation in Latvian law so far just on the basis of these publications.

Similarly as we indicated in the previous monograph *Contract Law in Latvia* concerning Latvian contract law, we observe that a separate publication in Latvian which comprehensively deals with Latvian tort law has also not been published. Despite the fact that Latvian legal scholars clearly distinguish between the law relating to contracts and the law relating to delicts (or torts, which is a more equivocal word in legal English for obligations not arising from contractual relationships), they treat tort law (similarly to contract law) as a part of the law of obligations but not as a separate sub-branch of civil law. This approach is dictated by the fact that tort law in Latvia is generally regulated under Civil Law as part of the law of obligations. This approach is followed in Latvian legal literature as there is no monograph or textbook in Latvian which comprehensively and separately deals with Latvian tort law (similarly as in the case of Latvian contract law) as a separate sub-branch of civil law. For instance, a well-known and recognized textbook (a so-called

9. Kārkliņš, J. Notion of Strict Liability in Private Law. University of Latvia Journal 'Law', 2017, No 10, pp. 175–199. Available also at https://www.journaloftheuniversityoflatvialaw.lu.lv/fileadmin/user_upload/lu_portal/projekti/journaloftheuniversityoflatvialaw/No10/J.Karklins.pdf.
10. Karklins, J. Third-parties as an Exclusion from Strict Liability, in: Legal Science: *Functions, Significance and Future in Legal Systems*, 16–18 Oct. 2019, Riga: Collection of research papers in conjunction with the 7th International Scientific Conference of the Faculty of Law of the University of Latvia. Riga: University of Latvia Press, 2020, pp. 376–382. Available also at https://www.apgads.lu.lv/fileadmin/user_upload/lu_portal/apgads/PDF/Juridiskas-konferences/ISCFLUL-7-2019/Book-iscflul.7.2_.pdf.
11. Mantrov, V. (2014) Is 142 Euro Equal to 350,000 Euro? The CJEU Interpretation of 'Personal Injury' and 'Injured Party' in EU Motor Insurance Law. European Journal of Risk Regulation. vol. 5, 399–406.
12. The above and other publications on Latvian contract law in English used for preparation of this monograph are mentioned in the selected bibliography.
13. Torgāns, K., Kārkliņš, J. Contract Law, in: Kerikmäe T., Joamets K., Pleps J., Rodiņa A., Berkmanas T., Gruodytė E. (eds.). (2017) *The Law of the Baltic States*. Cham: Springer, 298–304.

study monograph) written in Latvian by Kalvis Torgāns deals with the law of obligations,[14] one of whose parts covers tort law. Likewise, a similar approach is undertaken in the teaching of Latvian civil law at the Faculty of Law, University of Latvia, which is the oldest institution in Latvia for teaching law. For instance, legal courses are taught at the Faculty of Law, University of Latvia in fields such as *Law of Obligations. General Part* and *Law of Obligations. Special Part* as well as *Contract and Delict Problems*, where tort law and related problems are taught as part of these courses but not within a separate course.

Finally, several reservations should be made concerning the terminology employed in this monograph. During preparatory work, the co-authors were forced to make several choices concerning the language used in this monograph.

On the one hand, the co-authors use language which is as much as possible close to the official text of Latvian legal acts drafted in Latvian. In this regard, the difficulty was to comply with the terminology which is traditionally used in Europe but which in some situations is different from that used in Latvian legal acts, especially in the Civil Law, and echoed in Latvian legal literature. For instance, the monograph uses the term 'tort' for non-contractual civil obligations instead of the term 'delict' which would be more precise to describe the understanding of a non-contractual obligation in Latvian civil law as sharing Roman private law foundations (similarly as in the case of other continental European countries). Or the term 'animal' which is more regular noun than the direct translation of the Latvian legal term 'four-legged' or a quadruped (*kustonis* in Latvian corresponding to the Latin term *quadruplus*). In addition, the authors preferred to classify damage into pecuniary and non-pecuniary damage by following Latvian civil law literature, in that way avoiding the term 'moral damage' despite the fact that the Civil Law (wrongly in the opinion of the authors) uses such a term. Other terminological reservations concerning the use of specific terms are mentioned in the list of abbreviations *infra*.

On the other hand, the authors tried as far as possible to use generally accepted terminology. For instance, the term 'tortfeasor' was preferred due to the terminology of tort law instead of such terms as 'infringer' (employed in the official translation of the Civil Law) or 'injuring party'. Likewise, the term 'victim' was employed (also in the official translation of the Civil Law) instead of the term 'injured party'. In addition, the terms 'creditor' or 'debtor' were used depending on the context. Therefore, the term 'creditor' does not always cover the term 'victim' but the term 'debtor' covers the term 'tortfeasor'. Also, the term 'claim' should be understood from the substantive law standpoint by referring to a creditor's claim demanding something from the debtor based on the assertion of a right protected under substantive law. However, if the term 'claim' is used in connection with civil proceedings, for instance, stating that someone brought a claim to the court, in this situation, the term is perceived from a procedural standpoint. Consequently, the terms 'claimant' and 'defendant' refer to civil procedure law but not substantive law. Likewise, the term 'damage' was preferred instead of the term 'harm' and, therefore, the term 'damages' was used instead of the term 'losses' (though with certain exceptions, usually when the latter term is used in the official translation itself).

14. Torgāns, K. Saistību tiesības [Law of Obligations]. Otrais papildinātais izdevums [Second supplemented edition]. Rīga: Tiesu namu aģentūra, 2017.

## Preface

This monograph was prepared as the result of an initiative by the Institute of Legal Science of the Faculty of Law, University of Latvia, to contribute to the preparation of national monographs within the *International Law Encyclopaedia*. More information on the Institute may be found at the Institute's web-page available at https://www.jf.lu.lv/par-mums/juridiskas-zinatnes-instituts/; information on the Institute's projects is available at https://www.jf.lu.lv/petnieciba/projekti/.

# General Introduction

## §1. General Background of the Country

### I. Geography

*1.* Latvia (*Latvija* [lætviə] in Latvian; official title – the Republic of Latvia (*Latvijas Republika* in Latvian)) is a European country located in the north-eastern part of Europe. The territory of Latvia to the west and north-west lies on the shores of the Baltic Sea and the Gulf of Riga. Latvia is one of the three Baltic states[15] and simultaneously one of the Baltic Sea region countries. The official state language in Latvia is Latvian. Currently the population of Latvia is approximately 1.9 million inhabitants and has continuously been decreasing in recent years due to negative international migration and excess of deaths over births.[16] The Latvian population is more than one and a half times larger than the population of Estonia but at the same time one and a half times smaller than the population of Lithuania.

*2.* The land territory of Latvia occupies 64,573 km$^2$ – slightly less than the area of Lithuania but one and a half times larger than the area of Estonia, whose area is larger than that of the Netherlands. The neighbouring countries of Latvia by land are Estonia (also a sea border), Lithuania (also a sea border), Russia and Belarus. Sweden is the only one of Latvia's neighbouring countries with which Latvia has only a maritime border. The total length of Latvia's land border is 1,387 km, and the total maritime border is 498 km.[17]

*3.* Latvia is located in the temperate climate zone. Its climate is influenced by relatively flat terrain, proximity to the sea and air masses from the Atlantic Ocean.

15. Lithuania and Estonia are the others.
16. Bērziņš M.; Apsīte – Beriņa E., Eglīte P., Krišjāne Z., Kūle L. VI. Iedzīvotāji un apdzīvojums. Grām.: Latvija. Zeme, daba, tauta, valsts. Otrais laidiens. Rīga: Latvijas Universitāte, 2018, 495.lpp. Key economic data on Latvia available in English on the web-page of the OECD. OECD, Latvia, selected indicators for Latvia. Available at https://data.oecd.org/latvia.htm. Alternatively, different data about Latvia available in English on the web-page of the Central Statistical Bureau – the Latvian state institution responsible for statistics. Available at http://www.csb.gov.lv/en.
17. Centrālā statistikas pārvalde/Central Statistical Bureau of Latvia. Latvijas vide skaitļos 2019.gadā: klimata pārmaiņas, dabas resursi un vides kvalitāte/Environment of Latvia in figures: climate change, natural resources and environmental quality 2019. Rīga: Centrālā statistikas pārvalde/ Central Statistical Bureau of Latvia, 2020, 12.lpp. Available in Latvian and English at https:// admin.stat.gov.lv/system/files/publication/2020-12/Nr_22_Vides_raditaji_Latvija_2019_%2820_00 %29_LV_EN_0.pdf.

The climate is mild and humid with four separate seasons. In 2019, the mean daily air temperature in January, the coldest month of the year, is -4.0 °C, while in June, the warmest month, the mean daily air temperature is +18.6°C.[18] As noted in a recent academic study of Latvian soil, nature, nation and country, maritime (i.e., maritime influence) as a typical feature of the Baltic Sea region is characteristic of Latvia as well. A little more than 35% of the country's territory is closer than 50 km from the open sea or the shore of the Gulf of Riga.[19]

## II. History

*4.* Latvia's independence was proclaimed on 18 November 1918 by announcing that the sovereign power in Latvia had passed into the hands of the Latvian People's Council established the previous day.[20] The Latvian Constitution[21] was adopted almost four years later on 15 February 1922 and entered into force on 7 November 1922.[22] Latvia lost its independence after its inclusion in the USSR but regained its independence on 4 May 1990 after the collapse of the USSR when the Supreme Council of the Latvian Soviet Socialist Republic (SSR) adopted the Declaration 'On the Restoration of Independence of the Republic of Latvia'.[23]

## III. Political System

*5.* Under the constitutional system, Latvia is a parliamentary republic based on democratic values and the rule of law. The legal basis of the constitutional system in Latvia is framed by the Latvian Constitution (*Latvijas Republikas Satversme* in Latvian, *Satversme*).[24] As indicated above, the *Satversme* was adopted on 15 February 1922 and entered into force on 7 November 1922. The *Satversme* was restored into force on 4 May 1990 by the Supreme Council of the Latvian Socialist Soviet

18. *Ibid.*
19. Latvija. Zeme, daba, tauta, valsts. Otrais laidiens. [Latvia. Land, nature, people, country. Second edition] Nikodemus O., Kļaviņš M., Krišjāne Z., Zelčs V. (zin. red.). Rīga: Latvijas Universitātes Akadēmiskais apgāds, 2018, 15.lpp.
20. Šiliņš, J. Latvijas Republikas proklamēšana [Proclamation of the Republic of Latvia]. Nacionālā enciklopēdija [National Encyclopedia]. Available in Latvian at https://enciklopedija.lv/skirklis/113378-Latvijas-Republikas-proklam%C4%93%C5%A1ana.
21. For more information, *see* the next sub-paragraph of this chapter on the political system in Latvia.
22. Pleps, J., Plepa, D. Latvijas Republikas Satversme [Constitution of the Republic of Latvia]. Nacionālā enciklopēdija [National Encyclopedia]. Available in Latvian at https://enciklopedija.lv/skirklis/100866-Latvijas-Republikas-Satversme.
23. Latvijas Padomju Sociālistiskās Republikas Augstākās padomes deklarācija 'Par Latvijas Republikas neatkarības atjaunošanu' [Declaration of the Supreme Council of the Latvian Soviet Socialist Republic 'On the Restoration of Independence of the Republic of Latvia']. Adopted on 4 May. 1990, entered into force on 4 May. 1990.
24. Constitution of the Republic of Latvia. Official translation into English available on the official webpage of the State Language Centre at http://www.vvc.gov.lv/export/sites/default/docs/LRTA/Likumi/Constitution.doc.

Republic after the collapse of the Union of Soviet Socialist Republics (USSR). However, restoration of the *Satversme* took place gradually until its force was fully restored on 6 July 1993.[25]

*6.* An essential feature of the Latvian constitutional system is related to the fact that Latvia is a unitary country. It is traditionally divided into several historical regions such as *Kurzeme* (located in the western part of Latvia where it borders on Lithuania to the south), *Zemgale* (located in the central part of Latvia, bordering on Lithuania to the south as well), *Vidzeme* (in the central and eastern part of Latvia and bordering on Estonia to the north) and *Latgale* (located in the eastern part of Latvia, bordering on Russia and Belarus to the east and southeast). These historical regions, however, have no impact on the Latvian constitutional system but represent ethnographic, historical, and language dialect differences and are thus traditionally distinguished.

*7.* State management is shared by the central government and so-called derived public persons within the constitutional system of Latvia as reflected by the *Satversme* and legal acts adopted by the Parliament (*Saeima* in Latvian). Regulation of state management is included in a special law – the State Administration Structure Law.[26] This law defines the term 'public person', which comprises the Republic of Latvia as the initial legal person governed by public law as well as derived public persons. These acts are in line with the principles of public law.[27] By regulating the activities of public persons, this law distinguishes the Republic of Latvia, as the initial public person, which acts in the field of state administration through the intermediation of institutions of direct and indirect administration,[28] while derived public persons act in the field of state administration through the intermediation of institutions of indirect administration.[29] The competence of derived public persons, such as municipalities, is based on a separate legal act.[30]

*8.* Simultaneously, Latvian law allows the state itself (that is, the Republic of Latvia) and its established derived public persons to participate in civil law relationships as legal persons of public law simultaneously being civil law subjects.[31]

25. *See* Rodiņa, A., Kārkliņa, A. Constitutional Law and Constitutional Review, in: Kerikmäe et al, *supra* n. 10, *The Law of the Baltic States*. p. 192.
26. State Administration Structure Law. Official translation into English available on the official webpage of the State Language Centre at https https://vvc.gov.lv/image/catalog/dokumenti/State_Administration_Structure_Law.doc.
27. *Ibid.*, Art. 1(2).
28. *Ibid.*, Art. 4(1).
29. *Ibid.*, Art. 4(1).
30. E.g., the competence of municipalities in Latvia is established on the basis of the Law 'On Local Government' which, with subsequent amendments, has been in force for almost twenty-five years (adopted on 19 May. 1994, entered into force on 9 Jun. 1994). Official translation into English available on the official web-page of the State Language Centre at https://vvc.gov.lv/image/catalog/dokumenti/On_Local_Governments.doc.
31. For an overview of contracts concluded by the State and derived public persons, *see* Torgāns, K., Kārkliņš, J., Mantrov, V., Rasnačs, L. (2020), *supra* n. 4, p. 253 *et seq*.

*9.* Latvia has been active in integrating into international organizations at both the global and regional levels. Latvia has been a Member State of the World Trade Organization (WTO) since 1999 and a Member State of the Organisation for Economic Co-operation and Development (OECD) since 1 July 2016. Furthermore, Latvia joined the European Union (EU) as a Member State on 1 May 2004, together with the other two Baltic states and in addition to seven other countries. Likewise, Latvia has joined almost all significant international treaties, including those related to civil law.

## IV. Economic and Social Values

*10.* The *Satversme* states the values upon which the Republic of Latvia is established and operates:

> Latvia as a democratic, socially responsible and national state is based on the rule of law and on respect for human dignity and freedom; it recognises and protects fundamental human rights and respects ethnic minorities.[32]

*11.* This statement encapsulates, for example, the idea that Latvia is a socially responsible country required to ensure a minimum social protection standard. This idea is closely connected with the catalogue of fundamental rights and freedoms recognized by the *Satversme*. Specifically, Article 109 of the *Satversme* states that:

> Everyone has the right to social security in old age, for work disability, for unemployment and in other cases as provided by law.

The minimum social protection standard is ensured on the basis of other national legal acts, such as providing social allowances in certain cases and pensions under the prescribed conditions.

*12.* The Latvian economy is based on market economy principles. The country's economy may be considered as a small, open, export-oriented economy which due to this characteristic is rather vulnerable to external economic processes and world economic developments. In this regard, the OECD has pointed out that Latvia is a dynamic, small and open economy, but with a declining population and skills shortage.[33] A similar opinion was stated in Latvia's latest economic development report by noting that Latvia as a small open economy is sensitive to external shocks.[34] The ongoing COVID-19 pandemic is a good illustration of this situation. That is, until the COIVD-19 pandemic, economic growth had remained stable, exceeding the EU

32. Constitution of the Republic of Latvia, *supra* n. 24, preamble, para. 4.
33. OECD. Innovation, Agricultural Productivity and Sustainability in Latvia. Paris: OECD Publishing, 2019. Available in English at https://www.oecd.org/latvia/innovation-agricultural-productivity-and-sustainability-in-latvia-9789264312524-en.htm.
34. Ekonomikas ministrija [Ministry of Economy]. Latvijas ekonomiskās attīstības pārskats [Latvia's economic development report]. Rīga: Ekonomikas ministrija, 2020, 71.lpp. Available in Latvian at https://www.em.gov.lv/lv/media/4061/download.

average level. From 2011 to 2019, gross domestic product (GDP) grew on average at 3.3% annually.[35] However, the COVID-19 pandemic has significantly influenced the Latvian economy. According to the Ministry of Economics, in 2020, GDP in Latvia in 2020 could shrink by 5%–6% compared to 2019 but in reality it shrank just by 3.6%; however, economic growth, which was predicted as likely to resume in 2021, has taken place since the second quarter of 2020.[36]

## §2. Legal Systems

### I. Primacy of Legislation and Codification

*13.* The *primacy* of general principles of law and legal norms is *characteristic* of the Latvian legal system arising from the fact that Latvia is a civil-law country. This idea is reflected in the classification of sources of law in Latvia and explicitly admitted at the legislative level.

*14.* Latvian legal literature distinguishes permanent *sources of law* as being sources of generally binding character from auxiliary (or ancillary) sources of law or sources which do not have a generally binding character. Permanent sources of law cover normative acts, customary law (as far as this is allowed by normative acts) and general principles of law, whereas the second group consists of settled court practice, legal literature (or doctrine such as monographs, articles in scientific journals or conference proceedings, promotional works and the like), preparatory materials for normative legal acts, and so on.[37] This classification demonstrates that general principles of law and legal norms enjoy primacy over other sources of law. The same conclusion may be arrived at from sources of private law simultaneously being also sources of tort law. These sources include general principles of law, legal acts (laws) and other external normative legal acts, customary law, court practice and legal literature.[38]

*15.* At the legislative level, the Civil Law admits the supremacy of legislation by envisaging that the Civil Law is applicable to all legal issues to which its text or interpretation relates. Rights based on custom may neither set aside nor vary by law. Rights based on custom are applicable in those cases specified by law.[39]

*16.* Therefore, an enforcer of legal norms falling within private law in general or tort law in particular – such as state, municipal and court institutions – substantiates its decisions or rulings on the basis of general principles of law and legal

35. *Ibid.*, 11.lpp.
36. *Ibid.*, Ekonomikas ministrija [Ministry of Economy]. Latvijas ekonomiskās attīstības pārskats [Latvia's economic development report]. Rīga: Ekonomikas ministrija, 2021, 10.lpp. Available in Latvian at https://www.em.gov.lv/lv/media/12820/download.
37. Torgāns, K., Kārkliņš, J., Mantrov, V., Rasnačs, L. (2020), *supra* n. 4, p. 28.
38. *Ibid.*
39. Article 2 Civil Law (CL).

norms included in different normative acts, subject to the hierarchy of legal norms discussed in legal literature and envisaged by law.[40]

*17.* Generally accepted legal principles of civil law such as the good faith principle placed in the very first article of the Civil Law, the duty to act in compliance with moral principles (*labi tikumi* in Latvian), private autonomy of the parties and freedom of contract, are usually considered as such principles and applied by Latvian courts. Moreover, it is the stable practice of Latvian courts to use these legal principles in their reasoning in addition to written legal norms.

*18.* At the same time, it is not possible to undermine the role of general principles of law and settled court practice, which is increasingly taken into consideration by the Latvian courts. For instance, Latvian courts have established settled court practice in certain aspects in relation to contract law, such as unjust penalties. This was even more important before 2014 than nowadays because this settled court practice was used as a source for suppressing unjust penalties before the modernization of regulation of penalties finally took place in 2014. Another area of the special meaning of settled court practice in civil law relates to establishing the amount of non-pecuniary damage in relation to damage caused to the non-pecuniary interests of persons such as life, health or physical integrity in the case of a natural person or reputation in the case of a legal person.

*19.* The Latvian legislator is inclined to follow the *codification* approach, though not to the full extent. This approach takes the form that the Latvian legislator adopts codification for regulation of a significant branch of law. This is supplemented by legal norms scattered among other legal acts. For instance, the Civil Law is considered a codification of civil law in Latvia. However, the Civil Law is supplemented by other legal acts containing special norms which either almost fully replace a particular regulation (for instance, in the case of a labour contract); or substantially amend it (for instance, in the case of a carriage contract in the so-called carriage legal acts); or provide certain special rules (for instance, in the case of commercial purchase contracts, commercial commission contracts or commercial bailment contracts in commercial law; or conformity of the purchase object with the contract in the case of consumer protection law).

*20.* As regards the regulation of tort, the Civil Law contains the basic norm for compensation of damage caused by an infringement recognized under civil law, including torts[41] supplemented with regulation of typical torts.[42] In this sense, the Civil Law is viewed as a codification of tort regulation. At the same time, this regulation is supplemented by special regulation of specific torts in other legal acts such as torts in product liability, environmental law, and so on.

---

40. Torgāns, K., Kārkliņš, J., Mantrov, V., Rasnačs, L. (2020), *supra* n. 4, pp. 29–31.
41. Article 1635(1) CL.
42. Ch.19 Law of Obligations Part of the Civil Law.

## II. Position of the Judiciary

*21.* The *Satversme* establishes division of powers. Legislative power is vested in the *Saeima* and the people of Latvia,[43] although the Cabinet has certain legislative power within limits set out by the *Satversme*. Executive power is in the hands of the Cabinet, which consists of the Head of the Cabinet and Ministers.[44] Latvian courts execute judicial power on the basis of Articles 82–86 of the *Satversme*.

*22.* The court system in Latvia is generally established by the *Satversme* in Chapter VI under the title 'Courts'. Article 82 of the *Satversme* outlines the structure of the Latvian court system. This article states that in Latvia, court cases are to be heard by district (city) courts, regional courts and the Supreme Court, but in the event of war or a state of emergency, also by military courts. Article 85 of the *Satversme* deals separately with the Constitutional Court. This states that Latvia will have a Constitutional Court, which, within its jurisdiction as prescribed by law, reviews cases concerning conformity of laws with the Constitution, as well as other cases conferred by law within its jurisdiction. The Constitutional Court is entitled to declare laws or other enactments or parts thereof invalid. The *Saeima* confirms the appointment of judges to the Constitutional Court for a term set by law, with a majority of votes of not less than fifty-one members of the *Saeima*.

*23.* The law 'On Court Power' lays down further rules for the functioning of the Latvian court system. The first instance court is a city (district) court, which hears cases on the substance. There are two kinds of first instance courts: one covers the so-called general jurisdiction courts hearing civil and criminal cases at first instance and the second covers administrative courts hearing administrative cases; an appeal instance court, which is a regional court – there are six regional courts in Latvia with one for each region and a separate regional court in Riga and a separate administrative regional court – hearing administrative cases only. Regional courts hear a case on appeal by reviewing the case on its substance. The third instance court is a cassation instance court which hears cases on matters of law only. There is only one cassation instance court in Latvia, which is the Supreme Court. This consists of three departments, each hearing either civil or criminal or administrative cases. The Ministry of Justice has traditionally refused to support the idea of specialized courts, although the distribution of cases in courts usually takes place by considering the specialization of a particular judge. Furthermore, certain courts are appointed to hear certain categories of cases. An exception to the court system of three instances occurs in a few cases when a regional court hears a case as a first instance court and a cassation instance court – as an appeal instance court.

*24.* Military courts are further dealt with in a separate legal act called the Military Courts Law (*Karatiesu likums* in Latvian).[45] These courts are outside the system of three-instance courts and may be established only when an exceptional

43. Article 64 *Satversme*.
44. Article 55 *Satversme*.
45. Military Courts Law. No official translation into English available.

situation or war is declared. This law envisages establishing and terminating military courts, lays down rules for the jurisdiction and judges of military courts as well as public prosecutors and attorneys who may act in military courts. So far, these military courts have not been established in Latvia.

*25.* Latvia's Constitutional Court (*Satversmes tiesa* in Latvian) is considered to be outside the system of three-instance courts. However, it plays a significant role in the Latvian court system as it is a court of constitutional review. It adjudicates matters on the conformity of laws and other regulatory enactments with the *Satversme*. The Constitutional Court acts on the basis of a separate legal act called the Constitutional Court Law.[46] The Constitutional Court may annul a legal act adopted by the *Saeima*, the Cabinet or other institution which is contrary to the *Satversme* or international treaties binding on Latvia as well as a legal act on accession to an international treaty (signed or entered into by Latvian institutions) if its provisions do not conform with the *Satversme*.[47]

## III. Distinction Between Public and Private Law

*26.* Latvia follows the traditions of Roman law by classifying law into public and private law. At the same time, as will be discussed further, both areas of law interrelate with each other. The classification simultaneously refers to both persons (i.e., legal persons of public law and private law) and legal norms falling within public or private law.

*27.* As regards persons, Latvian law distinguishes between legal persons of public law and private law. Unlike regulation in the other Baltic states, where this distinction is based on norms of civil codification, in Latvia, this arises from a legal act which regulates state management.[48] Indeed, the State Administration Structure Law affirms that a public person is the Republic of Latvia as the initial legal person governed by public law and derived public persons. Derived public persons would include municipalities, state-established universities, the Bank of Latvia, the Public Utilities Commission, the Latvian Academy of Sciences, the Latvian Council of Sworn Advocates, and others.[49] These persons are required to act in line with the principles of public law.[50] Likewise, legal persons in public law may participate in private law relationships insofar as the law permits.[51] At the same time, this Law

46. Constitutional Court Law. Official translation into English is available on the official web-page of the State Language Centre at http://www.vvc.gov.lv/export/sites/default/docs/LRTA/Likumi/Constitutional_Court_Law.doc.
47. For the competence of the Constitutional Court, *see* Art. 16 Constitutional Court Law. For an overview of the Latvian Constitutional Court, *see* Rodiņa A., Kārkliņa A. Constitutional Law and Constitutional Review, in: Kerikmäe et al., *supra* n. 10. *The Law of the Baltic States*. pp. 200–204.
48. I.e., State Administration Structure Law, *supra* n. 26.
49. Briede J., Danovskis E., Kovaļevska A. Administratīvās tiesības. Mācību grāmata. Otrais izdevums [*Administrative Law. Textbook. Second edition*]. Rīga: Tiesu namu aģentūra, 2021, 44–47.lpp.
50. State Administration Structure Law, *supra* n. 26, Art. 1(1).
51. *Ibid.*, Ch. XI.

declares that a private individual is a natural person, a legal person governed by private law or an association of such persons.[52]

*28.* Private law is further distinguished into three sub-branches of law such as civil law, private international law, and commercial law.[53] There are general sub-branches of civil law such as family law, inheritance law, law of things (i.e., property law), and law of obligations supplemented by special sub-branches such as consumer protection law, insurance law, labour law, intellectual property law, and so on. Latvian civil law also distinguishes special subjects requiring special regulation, such as the consumer in consumer protection law; the employee in labour law; and the merchant in commercial law.

*29.* Public law comprises substantive law such as administrative law, criminal law, constitutional law, public international law, tax law, social security law, as well as procedural law such as civil procedure law, administrative procedure law, and criminal procedure law.

*30.* It is possible to identify the influence of an interrelation between public law and private law in certain situations. On the one hand, public law influences private law relationships in the case of public registers (for instance, in the case of merchants in commercial law; immovables; intellectual property objects); licensing (for instance, construction law, insurance law); supervision of state institutions (for instance, labour law; consumer protection law; construction law); or in other matters, for instance, compensation of damage caused in torts when the tortfeasor commits a criminal offence. On the other hand, regulation of contract law influences public law contracts. Indeed, the State Administration Structure Law states that contracts governed by public law must be concluded in written form in conformity with the Civil Law and conforming to restrictions laid down in legal acts.[54]

## IV. Sources of Private Law in General and of Tort Law in Particular

*31.* The understanding of sources of tort law in Latvia is similar to the understanding of private law sources in general[55] and contract law in particular. In such a way, it is possible to identify international law and national law.

*32.* As regards *international law*, several international treaties relating to private law are binding on Latvia. A few of these international treaties refer to tort law. One example is the Convention of 4 May 1971 on the Law Applicable to Traffic Accidents. This international treaty falling within private international law deals with the

52. *Ibid.*, Art. 1(11).
53. Mantrovs, V. Civiltiesības [Civil Law]. Nacionālā enciklopēdija [National Encyclopedia]. Available in Latvian at https://enciklopedija.lv/skirklis/5991-civilties%C4%ABbas.
54. Article 12(2) State Administration Structure Law, *supra* n. 26.
55. For discussion of the understanding of sources of law, *see* Sub-ch.1 of this chapter, *supra*.

applicable law in road traffic accidents and, therefore, indirectly relates to tort law. Latvia acceded to this international treaty on 15 October 2000.[56]

*33.* Sources of private law at the *national* level may be found mainly in legal acts. In addition, regulations of the Cabinet, binding regulations of a municipality and also other legal acts feature among these sources.

*34.* The Civil Law as the main codification of private law contains general regulation of tort law. In this way, the Civil Law contains a basic norm for every infringement of a right to a civil law object, including infringements recognized as non-contractual obligations, that is, torts.[57] Furthermore, Chapter 19 of the Law of Obligations Part of the Civil Law contains different typical (i.e., nominated or normatively regulated) torts commencing with bodily injury;[58] continuing with personal freedom,[59] reputation and dignity,[60] chastity;[61] and committing damage to property[62] and, finally, quasi-torts relating to damage caused by throwing, pouring or falling [63] and damage caused by animals[64] as well as – in certain situations – unjust enrichment.[65] Other legal acts contain special regulation which derogate from general regulation of torts included in the Civil Law. One may mention several significant legal acts such as the *Law on the Safety of Goods and Services*, the *Law on Liability for Defects of Goods and Services*, the *Competition Law*, the *Motor Insurance Law*, and the *Law on Construction Law*. These and other legal acts are discussed in the present monograph.

## §3. Function of the Law of Torts: Indemnification; Prevention; Sanction

*35.* As already stated concerning terminology about the use of the term 'tort', from the terminological standpoint of Latvian private law, it would be appropriate to use the term 'delict' (*delictum* in Latin) instead of the term 'tort'.[66] This conclusion is based on the fact that Latvian private law is based on the traditions of Roman

56. Convention of 4 May. 1971 on the Law Applicable to Traffic Accidents. Status table. Available at https://www.hcch.net/en/instruments/conventions/status-table/?cid=81.
57. Article 1635(1) CL.
58. Articles 2347–2351 CL.
59. Article 2352 CL.
60. Article 2352.[1] CL.
61. *Ibid.*
62. Articles 2354–2357 CL.
63. Articles 2358–2362 CL.
64. Articles 2363–2368 CL.
65. Article 2369 *et seq* CL.
66. From the terminology point of view, it should be noted that the co-authors of the DCFR also discusses the use of both terms yet preferring the term 'non-contractual liability' as a neutral term (Bar, C. von, Clive, E., Schulte-Nölke, H., Beale, H., Herre, J., Huet, J., Storme, M., Swann, S., Varul, P., Veneziano, A., Zoll, F. (eds.). *Principles, Definitions and Model Rules of European Private Law Draft Common Frame of Reference* (DCFR) [DCFR], pp. 26, 35, 2978 *et seq*. Available at https://www.law.kuleuven.be/personal/mstorme/european-private-law_en.pdf).

law and continental Europe rather than common law. However, due to the terminology used in the present series of monographs, the term 'tort' is employed, yet in the understanding of 'delict'.

*36.* As a general rule, similarly to other European countries,[67] the function of Latvian tort law is related to its *compensatory* nature in both pecuniary and non-pecuniary damage. This means that tort law should protect the *status quo* in society.[68] This rule is encapsulated in Article 1635(1) of the Civil Law, being the basic norm for civil liability in Latvian civil law, including tort law.[69] Specifically, this provision refers to a right of the victim 'to claim satisfaction from the infringer' liable for the infringement, therefore, it generally emphasizes the compensatory nature of Latvian civil law, which also covers tort law. In this regard, it is indicated in Latvian civil law literature that the aim of tort law is related to compensation of damage caused to the victim as the result of a tort in addition to the related function of ensuring the existence of the legal order.[70]

*37.* Likewise, the compensatory nature is clearly seen in preconditions of civil liability which in sum relates to compensating the victim of an infringement.[71]

*38.* Similarly, Latvian civil law scholars have indicated that the main task of civil liability is not to punish tortfeasors, but as far as possible to prevent the consequences of infringements, i.e., to place the victim in the proprietary situation they were in before or in the state in which they would be if the infringement had not occurred.[72] A similar view was expressed by Professor Kalvis Torgāns by indicating that the punishment function is not characteristic of civil law, though a certain punishing function may be observed in the case of civil liability. He goes on to discuss

67. DCFR, *supra* n. 66, p. 937.
68. *Ibid.*, p. 63.
69. A different opinion is expressed concerning the nature of the regulation included in Art. 1635(1) Civil Law by indicating that it covers only torts (Čakste K. Civiltiesības [Civil Law]. Lekcijas [Lectures]. Grām.: Čakste K. Civiltiesības. Lekcijas. Raksti [Civil Law. Lectures. Articles]. R.: Zvaigzne ABC, 2011, 192.lpp.). However, this opinion is not supported in modern Latvian civil-law literature by linking this provision with a tort and a contractual infringement, i.e., understanding this provision in the meaning of a basic norm for civil liability (Balodis K. Ievads civiltiesībās [*Introduction to Civil Law*]. Rīga: Zvaigzne ABC, 2007, 135.lpp.).
70. Torgāns, K.; Kārkliņš, J.; Bitāns, A. Līgumu un deliktu problēmas Eiropas Savienībā un Latvijā [*Problems of Contracts and Delicts in the European Union and Latvia*]. Rīga: Tiesu namu aģentūra, 2017, 263.lpp.
71. For preconditions of civil liability in general and those applicable in Latvian tort law, *see* Pt. I of this monograph *infra*.
72. Kārkliņš, J. Latvijas līgumtiesību modernizācijas galvenie virzieni [*The Main Directions of Modernization of Latvian Contract Law*]. Promocijas darbs [PhD Thesis]. Rīga, 2006, 86., 124–125.lpp. Available in Latvian at https://dspace.lu.lv/dspace/bitstream/handle/7/5070/17797Janis_Karklins_2007.pdf?sequence=1.

the example of a penalty which may be viewed as a punishment.[73] In addition, it is also possible to identify the function of sanctions (i.e., punishment) in those cases when punitive damages are envisaged.[74]

*39.* At the same time, Torgāns indicated that the main aim of civil law is to ensure *equivalence* of pecuniary relations.[75] This consideration underlines the compensatory nature of tort law as discussed above.

*40.* Latvian tort law does not generally recognize the *preventive* function of tort law unless prevention is considered within the content of the compensatory nature discussed above. As stated in a comparative study of Latvian and American approaches to contract law: '[t]he approach in European legal theory is that liability (or sanctions) may have not only a compensatory but also a preventative function in private law'.[76] Torgāns continues this idea by noting that there exists individual prevention in respect of a single law infringer and general prevention in respect of potential law infringers.[77] At the same time, another – more cautious – opinion was expressed in Latvian civil law specifically concerning the preventive function of tort law. This was that the preventive function of civil liability concerning tort 'is limited to the determination of tort liability itself, since payment of compensation may in itself cause an individual and general deterrent effect'.[78]

*41.* Therefore, the preventive function of civil law in general and tort law in particular may also be distinguished in certain cases. Features of the preventive function of tort law may be recognized in the case of punitive damages referred to in paragraph 38 *supra*.

*42.* Another example could be damages which are likely to occur in the future so the victim may claim security. This is nothing extraordinary in European civil law as such a possibility is explicitly recognized in the DCFR.[79] In Latvia, Article 1771 of the Civil Law would be applicable here. This Article distinguishes two types of damages depending on the moment when they arise. This Article provides that:

73. Torgāns, K. (2018), *supra* n. 11, 155–156.lpp.
74. For a detailed discussion of punitive damages in Latvia, *see* Pt. VI, Ch. 7, Sub-ch. 3 of this monograph *infra*.
75. Torgāns, K. [Commentary of Article 1635 of the Civil Law], ram.: Latvijas Republikas Civillikuma komentāri. Saistību tiesības (1401–2400.p.) [Commentary to the Civil Law of the Republic of Latvia. Law of Obligations (Arts 1401–2400)]. Prof. K.Torgāna zinātniskajā redakcijā. Rīga: Mans ı¯pašums, 2000, 144.lpp.
76. Torgans, K., Bushaw, A. Some Comparative Aspects of Contract Law in Civil and Common Law Systems. International Legal Perspectives, 2001–2002, vol. 12, p. 67.
77. Torgāns, K. (2018), *supra* n. 11, 155–156.lpp.
78. Kubilis, J. Latvijas deliktu tiesību modernizācijas galvenie virzieni [*Main directions for Modernization of Latvian Tort Law*]. Promocijas darbs [PhD Thesis]. Riga, 2016, 30.lpp. Available in Latvian at https://dspace..lu.lv/dspace/bitstream/handle/7/34956/298-57104-Kubilis_Janis_jk07041.pdf?sequence=1&isAllowed=y.
79. DCFR, *supra* n. 66, p. 2998 *et seq*.

> [l]osses may be either such losses as have already arisen, or such losses as are anticipated; in the former case, they give rise to a right to compensation, but in the latter case, to a right to security.

*43.* As one may observe from this provision, the Civil Law grants a potential victim the right to security to be claimed in court from the alleged tortfeasor. This provision, however, is a substantive law norm, so that application of this right should be based on the civil procedure rules in the CPL. From the standpoint of substantive law, a victim as creditor has a claim for indemnification of anticipated damages.

*44.* The right to compensation of damages that may occur in the future should be distinguished from the similar institute of security of claim.[80] A claim will be secured by a judge or a court if there are reasonable grounds to believe that enforcement of the court judgment in the case may become problematic or impossible.[81] However, if the right to compensation of damages that may occur in the future is based on substantive law and applies to damages only, security of claim is based on procedural rules and is applied in any civil case.

## §4. Relationship Between Torts and Criminal Law

*45.* From the standpoint of private law, tort law has the most important relationship with criminal law. This relationship arises when conduct either in the form of an activity (more frequently) or inactivity (rarely) is criminalized and, in turn, causes damage to the protected lawful interests of a legal subject. As indicated in the practice summary of cases on fraud (but it may be applied as a general rule):

> [l]iability under private law and public law are not mutually subordinated. The fact that a person has been or may be held civilly or commercially liable for an offence does not mean that the offence cannot be considered a criminal or administrative offence as well.[82]

*46.* The term 'legal subject' referred to in the previous paragraph is understood in Latvian private law broadly by covering natural persons, legal persons of either public law or private law, and also partnerships which enjoy certain legal capacity.[83]

*47.* Neither the Civil law nor any other legal act provides either an exhaustive or nonexhaustive list of situations when particular conduct may lead to application simultaneously of criminal liability and tort law. The possibility of such situations

80. Article 137(1) CPL.
81. *Ibid.*
82. Latvijas Republikas Augstākā tiesa. Tiesu prakse lietās par krāpšanu [*Court Summary in Cases on Fraud*]. Riga, 2008/2009, 9.lpp. Available in Latvian at https://www.at.gov.lv/files/uploads/files/docs/summaries/2009/tp_krapsana.doc.
83. Balodis, K. (2007), *supra* n. 69, 73.lpp.

is based on whether preconditions of civil liability may be established in the case of a particular tort. In this regard, the court summary on a claim for non-pecuniary damage states that:

> [e]very criminal offence also causes moral [i.e. non-pecuniary damage – authors' remark] damage to a person. This is related to moral satisfaction, i.e. when a person receives a punishment prescribed by law for a criminal offence. Whether a person is entitled to material compensation for non-pecuniary damage is a matter for assessment. In order to establish the victim's right to material compensation, it is necessary to establish a causal link between criminal activities and the non-pecuniary damage suffered, i.e. whether such damage has been caused for which material compensation is due. The victim has the right to claim satisfaction from the tortfeasor, insofar as he or she may be held at fault for such act.[84]

*48.* However, it might be difficult in certain cases to distinguish whether the tortfeasor's activities liable for damage caused may simultaneously lead to criminal liability if it is possible to establish the conditions set out in the respective article of the Criminal Law in relation to a particular criminal offence. It is emphasized in Latvian legal literature that several criminal offences such as theft,[85] robbery,[86] fraud,[87] and misappropriation[88] as well as arbitrariness[89] (*patvarība* in Latvian) may contain evaluation of the conduct of a tortfeasor (a person who committed a civil offence) which is based on actions governed by civil law, such as conclusion or fulfilment of a contract, issuance of a power of attorney, and similar.[90]

*49.* In order to determine whether such actions may also lead to application of criminal law rules, the court summary on fraud prepared by the Supreme Court characterized a method for distinguishing fraud as a criminal offence from a tort based on rules of civil liability. The characterization of this method is worth quoting in full:

> Fraud is a criminal offence that is important to distinguish from a civil tort [such a term undoubtedly is inaccurate from the standpoint of Latvian law as a tort could be only based on civil law – authors' remark]. [..] Considering the legal nature of fraud, a person transferring property or rights to property to a fraudster is not aware of the criminal nature of the offence but perceives it as

84. Latvijas Republikas Augstākā tiesa. Tiesu prakse par morālā kaitējuma kompensāciju kriminālprocesā. Rīga, 66.lpp. Available in Latvian at https://www.at.gov.lv/files/uploads/files/docs/petijumi/tiesu%20prakse%20moralais%20kaitejums_an.doc.
85. Articles 175, 180 Criminal Law.
86. Articles 176 Criminal Law.
87. Articles 177–178, 180 Criminal Law.
88. Articles 179–180 Criminal Law.
89. Article 279 Criminal Law.
90. Leja, M. Krāpšanas un piesavināšanās norobežošana no civiltiesiska delikta [*Separation of Fraud and Misappropriation from Civil Tort*]. Jurista Vārds, 2018, Nr.11; Smans, A. Civiltiesiskās un krimināltiesiskās atbildības savstarpējā mijiedarbība un nošķiršana [*Interaction and Separation of Civil and Criminal Liability*]. Jurista Vārds, 2018, Nr.11.

> a civil or commercial relationship. The [liable] persons often use civil law instruments to commit fraudulent activities – in writing, orally or implicitly conclude contracts, or to engage in activities that externally appear to be lawful transactions. Actions which are considered fraudulent from a criminal law standpoint may be regarded as improper performance of a contractual obligation, evasion from fulfilment of obligations, etc. from the standpoint of a civil or commercial law. Punishing a person for a civil or commercial tort [*see* the reservation in the first sentence of this quote – authors' remark] the previous remark – or improper performance of a contractual obligation, as well as the possibility of such punishment, does not exclude a person's criminal liability for the committed fraud. At the same time, it should be noted that a civil tort does not in itself mean that a person has also committed a criminal offence. In order to have grounds for finding a person guilty of fraud, it is not enough to establish a breach of duties imposed by the contract – an offence may be declared criminal if all the objective and subjective features of the composition of the offence are established.[91]

*50.* Therefore, as one may observe from the quote above supported by Latvian court practice and Latvian legal literature, Latvian tort law is based on a presumption that application of criminal law and tort law is based on different legal rules. Consequently, civil liability arising from torts and criminal liability are independent from each other and for this reason both types of liability should be established separately.

*51.* At the same time, the Civil Law itself points to an interrelation between tort law and criminal law in certain cases. Indeed, one of the grounds for establishing a solidary (i.e., joint and several) obligation on the basis of law covers a jointly committed criminal offence.[92] Article 1675 of the Civil Law states that if a criminal offence has been committed jointly by more than one person, they shall be solidarily liable for losses caused thereby. Likewise, establishing a criminal offence in the cases prescribed by law simultaneously leads to a presumption of the existence of non-pecuniary damage. In this regard, the Civil Law envisages that:

> [i]f unlawful acts [..] are expressed as criminal offences against a person's life, health, morals, inviolability of gender, freedom, honour, dignity or against the family, or minors, it is presumed that the person who suffered the harm as a result of such acts has been done moral injury.

---

91. Latvijas Republikas Augstākā tiesa. Tiesu prakse lietās par krāpšanu [*Court Summary of Cases on Fraud*]. Riga, 2008/2009, 9–10.lpp. Available in Latvian at https://www.at.gov.lv/files/uploads/files/docs/summaries/2009/tp_krapsana.doc. *See also* in this regard Leja M. Krāpšanas aktuālie jautājumi Latvijas un ārvalstu tiesībās. Rīga: Tiesu namu aģentūra, 2013.
92. Article 1674 CL.

Furthermore, default by a debtor is established *per se* when the debtor has gained possession of property by criminal or generally illegal means.[93] Finally, if a subordinate commits a tort pursuant to the orders of his or her supervisor, the former shall not be held liable, if the act is not itself criminal.[94]

*52.* In the practice of the Latvian courts, damage caused as the result of a tort is compensated to the victim most frequently in criminal proceedings concerning homicide,[95] bodily injuries,[96] and damage caused due to a violation of traffic rules[97].[98]

*53.* However, the mere fact that the Criminal Procedure Law allows a claim in compensation for damage caused by performing a criminal offence within criminal proceedings (either in the pre-court proceedings or reviewing a criminal case in a court) does not contradict the conclusion reached in the preceding paragraph.[99] This is based on the fact that the Criminal Procedure Law provides for an alternate possibility to claim damages caused in addition to the possibility to bring a claim within civil procedure in a court of general jurisdiction. However, the mere possibility to claim compensation for damages caused in both proceedings cannot lead to double restitution, as justly claimed in Latvian legal literature.[100]

*54.* The same applies to the fact that civil proceedings may be stayed due to criminal (or administrative) proceedings. As the CPL provides, the court will stay in court proceedings if examination of the case is not possible prior to the deciding of another case which is required to be examined under civil, criminal or administrative procedures.[101] This provision refers to the duty of the court to suspend court proceedings if it is established as impossible to decide the given civil case until a criminal case has first been dealt with.[102] As stated in Latvian civil law literature in this regard, it is appropriate to stay civil proceedings if a court ruling in a criminal case may affect civil liability according to the claim submitted in particular court

93. Article 1652(1) CL.
94. Article 1638 CL.
95. Article 116 *et seq* Criminal Law.
96. Article 125 *et seq* Criminal Law.
97. Article 260 *et seq* Criminal Law. *See* in this regard Kaitējuma kompensācijas cietušajam noziedzīgā nodarījumā, kas saistīts ar ceļu satiksmes noteikumu un transportlīdzekļu ekspluatācijas noteikumu pārkāpšanu, izlemšana kriminālprocesā [*Criminal Proceedings for Compensation of a Victim of a Criminal Offence Related to a Violation of Traffic Rules and Vehicle Operation Regulations*]. Available in Latvian at https://www.at.gov.lv/files/uploads/files/6_Judikatura/Tiesu_prakses_apkopojumi/2020/Apkopojums_OCTA_lietas_kp_cp.docx.
98. The list of such cases is indirectly testified by a court summary on claim for non-pecuniary damage where these cases are the most frequent in which damages are awarded (*see* Latvijas Republikas Augstākā tiesa). Tiesu prakse par morālā kaitējuma kompensāciju kriminālprocesā. Rīga, 66.lpp. https://www.at.gov.lv/files/uploads/files/docs/petijumi/tiesu%20prakse%20moralais%20kaitejums_an.doc).
99. Article 350–353 Criminal Procedure Law.
100. Smans, A. (2018), *supra* n. 90.
101. Article 214(5) CPL.
102. Osis M., Rozenbergs J., Torgāns K. Komentārs par Civilprocesa likuma 214.pantu. Grām.: Civilprocesa likuma komentāri. I daļa (1–28.nodaļa). Otrais papildinātais izdevums [Commentary on

proceedings.[103] In this regard, it is important to note that a court ruling or decision with a similar effect in a criminal case is binding on a court examining the case involving the civil liability of the person regarding whom the relevant ruling was made, only with respect to the issue of whether a criminal act or failure to act occurred and whether such has been committed or respectively been allowed by the same person.[104]

## §5. Relationship Between Contractual and Delictual or Tortious Responsibility; Does the *Non Cumul* Rule apply? What About Pre-Contractual Liability?

*55.* The principle of *non-cumul des responsabilités* is known in French law designated to treat contractual and tortious liability as distinct liability types. A modern formulation of the principle of non-cumulation consists in saying that a creditor under a contractual obligation cannot, even if there would be such an interest, invoke against the debtor in that obligation rules of tort.[105] There are no traces, however, that French civil law influenced Latvian civil law.[106] Therefore, it is not possible to establish direct application of this principle in Latvian civil law. However, this does not mean that it is not possible to analyse whether a similar approach is (not) taken by Latvian civil law and court practice.

*56.* Latvian civil law admits the relationship between contractual and tortious responsibility. This is also discussed in Latvian civil law literature by viewing the relationship from the standpoint of several aspects.

*57.* The situation in Latvian civil law concerning the distinction between contractual and tortious liability is *twofold.*

*58.* On the one hand, Latvian civil law treats contractual liability and tortious liability as *distinct* liability types as each of these are based on different (though largely similar) rules. Therefore, it is necessary to establish whether particular damage is caused either on the basis of contractual or tortious liability model in order to apply a set of rules intended for this type of liability.

---

Article 214 of the Civil Procedure Law. In: *Commentary to the Civil Procedure Law.* Part I (Chapters 1 to 28). Second supplemented edition]. Sagatavojis autoru kolektīvs prof. K.Torgāna zinātniskajā redakcijā. Rīga: Tiesu namu aģentūra, 2016, 606 lpp. *et seq*; *see also* Kubilis, J. Tiesvedības apturēšana civillietā sakarā ar krimināllietu [*Suspension of Court Proceedings in Civil Case In Relation with Criminal Case*]. Jurista Vārds, 2018, Nr.11.

103. Kubilis, J. (2018), *supra* n. 102, Nr.11.

104. Article 96(3) CPL.

105. Faure-Abbad M. Ce que l'on appelle en France le principe du non-cumul des responsabilités contractuelle et délictuelle. In Memoria di Paolo Maria Vecchi/Giornata di studio Le frontiere mobile della responsabilità contrattuale Università degli Studi Roma Tre, Apr 2015, Rome, Italie. Available at https://hal.archives-ouvertes.fr/hal-02114778/document.

106. Torgāns, K.; Kārkliņš, J.; Mantrov, V.; Rasnačs, L. (2020), *supra* n. 4, p. 27.

*59.* On the other hand, Latvian civil law does not preclude a choice by a creditor (e.g., a victim in the case of a tort) to choose whether a particular claim for compensation of damage would be based on a contractual or tortious liability model, if such choice is permitted at all.

> For instance, the Latvian courts reviewed a dispute involving breach of the confidentiality clause in a contract which resulted in illegal transfer of a trade secret to a third person. The question arose whether such a claim may be considered under the rules of contractual liability because of breach of contract or alternatively as a tort under tort law as an act of unfair competition (or currently also within *sui generis* regulation of trade secrets). The claim itself was brought on the basis of tort law, qualifying this dispute as an act of unfair competition and, consequently, as a tort. An appellate instance court three times revoked the decision of the first instance court. The claimant withdrew the claim while the first instance court was reviewing the issue for the fourth time, thus leaving this matter without a final decision by the Latvian courts. However, this case demonstrates that the Latvian courts were actually willing to respect a creditor's choice in this case if such a choice is permitted under Latvian civil law.[107]

*60.* However, certain situations could arise when it is difficult to qualify which liability regime – either contractual or tortious – should be applied. The Civil Law does not provide any rules in this regard, so that such determination in the case of doubt would have to be carried out on a case-by-case basis. Latvian civil law literature is familiar with such situations as they are discussed from the standpoint of the applicable legal regime. For instance, in this particular regard, Konstantīns Čakste discusses the situation when a person who breaks a window should be liable on the basis of tort liability, but if a tenant damages or breaks something in the stairwell of an apartment building, for instance, breaks a window, then a claim for damages may be made against the tenant either on the basis of the rent contract or tort.[108]

## §6. Protected Interests. Are All Interests Equally Protected? Are Subjective Rights More Protected Than Others?

*61.* Latvian civil law in general and tort law in particular equally protect all lawful interests. Therefore, Latvian tort law does not distinguish between different protected interests from the standpoint of recognition of their protection. Indeed, Article 1635(1) Civil Law states that:

> [e]very delict [tort in the terminology used in this monograph – authors' remark], that is, every wrongful act *per se,* as a result of which harm has been

107. Judgment of the Civil Case Panel for the Supreme Court of the Republic of Latvia of 7 May. 2014 in Case PAC – 1180/2014 (C04154813). Unpublished.
108. Čakste, K. (2011), *supra* n. 69, 97.lpp.

caused (also moral injury), shall give the person who suffered harm therefrom the right to claim satisfaction from the infringer, insofar as he or she may be held at fault for such act.

*62.* As one may observe from this provision, the Civil Law protects all lawful interests concerning tangible and intangible legal objects on an equal basis.

*63.* However, the Civil Law provides simplified rules for compensation of damage in the case of violation of certain lawful interests. Two main situations should be mentioned in this regard. One situation refers to the presumption of non-pecuniary damage in the case of certain illegal activities listed on the basis of *numerus clausus.*[109] These activities include damage arising from criminal offences against a person's life, health, morals, inviolability of gender, freedom, honour, dignity or against the family or minors.[110] The second situation refers to designated (i.e., normatively regulated) torts providing certain claims to designated creditors against designated debtors, i.e., tortfeasors.[111] It should be noted that a different liability regime – either fault-based liability or strict liability[112] – may be imposed depending on a particular claim. [113]

109. Article 1635 (3) Civil Law.
110. *Ibid.*
111. Ch. 19 *Law of Obligations*. Part of the Civil Law.
112. For a discussion of these liability regimes in Latvian tort law, *see* Pt. 1, Ch. 1 of this monograph *infra*.
113. *Ibid.*

# Part I. Liability for One's Own Acts

## Chapter 1. General Principles

### §1. Unlawfulness and Fault

*64.* Article 1402 of the Civil Law provides that one of the founding grounds (*causa efficiens*) for establishing obligation rights is an unlawful act in the form of a tort as prescribed in that Article. A distinction between contractual and tortious liability may be particularly important in the context of the amount of compensation and assessment of fault because in the case of breach of a contractual obligation, usually it is not necessary to establish the debtor's fault in order to establish the obligation to compensate the damage.[114]

*65.* The purpose of regulation of tort law is to create exceptions to the general principle that the risk of damage should be borne by each person individually (*casum sentit dominus*). In other words, imposition on another person of the effects of infringement of a right (reimbursement of damage) is an exception which applies when a number of conditions laid down by law are satisfied. This is also determined in the third sentence of Article 92 of the *Satversme*, which states that 'Everyone, where his rights are violated without basis, has a right to commensurate compensation.' This Article prescribes a general rule of tort law: Any damage caused by an unlawful act must be compensated. This is precisely reflected in Article 1635 of the Civil Law,[115] which is considered to be the pillar of Latvian tort law.[116]

114. Brants, E. Vainas elementi līgumiskās atbildības piemērošanā [*Elements of fault in Application of Contractual Liability*]. Grām.: Starptautisko un Eiropas Savienības tiesību piemērošana nacionālajās tiesās. Latvijas Universitātes 78.starptautiskās zinātniskās konferences rakstu krājums [*Application of the International and European Union law in the National Courts. Collection of research papers of the 78th International Scientific Conference of the University of Latvia*]. Rīga: LU Akadēmiskais apgāds, 2020, 272., 285 lpp.

115. Torgāns, K., Kārkliņš, J., Bitāns, A. (2017), *supra* n. 70, 263–264.lpp.

116. Sinaiskis, V. Latvijas civiltiesību apskats. Lietu tiesības. Saistību tiesības [*Review of Latvian Civil Law. Property Law. Law of Obligations*]. Rīga: Latvijas Juristu biedrība, 1996, 148 lpp.; Strazdiņš, Ģ. Vispārējais zaudējumu atlīdzības prasījuma pamats delikta un saistības pārkāpuma gadījumā [*General Basis for the Claim for Damage in the Event of a Contractual Infringement and Tort*]. Jurista Vārds, 2018, Nr.6.

*66.* Article 1635(1) of the Civil Law postulates that:

> [e]very delict, that is, every wrongful act per se, as a result of which harm has been caused (also moral [i.e. non-pecuiary – authors' remark] injury), shall give the person who suffered the harm therefrom the right to claim satisfaction from the infringer, insofar as he or she may be held at fault for such act.

*67.* Under the cited provision, the preconditions of the tort concept generally are as follows: (1) an infringement of rights as a consequence of conduct in the form of an act or omission; (2) the unlawful nature of the conduct in the objective sense, that is, violation of a legal provision (in the case of action – in a broad sense; in the case of omission – in a narrow sense[117]) as such; (3) the unlawfulness of the conduct in the subjective sense, that is, attribution of the conduct to fault, or the fact that it is dependent on the will of the tortfeasor; it is sufficient that the tortfeasor did not apply the care and due diligence required by the legal order for the purpose of making him liable for the consequences of his act or omission.[118] Thus, fault-based tortious liability is the main concept of Latvian tort law. As regards the second criterion from the standpoint of modern civil law by considering the good faith principle enshrined under Article 1 of the Civil Law, misuse of rights (for example, where a right is exercised with the intention of harming another person) means that the rightholder has no vested interest in justifying exercise of rights formally inherent to him.[119] Consequently, in this case, such a person may be obliged to compensate for damage caused by an act which is only seemingly lawful. However, the concept of tortious liability ceases to exist where objective rights permit a related act (for example, permitted self-defence[120]), or the injured person has consented to do so,[121] or a person only exercises a right to which he is entitled.[122]

*68.* In explaining the requirements for tortious liability arising from Article 1635(1) of the Civil Law, the most recent legal literature[123] and court practice[124] generally lay down three cumulative preconditions: (1) unlawful and unjustifiable conduct by the tortfeasor, which, only in cases specified by law, excludes assessment from the fault standpoint; (2) the existence of damage in a particular amount (quantifiable damage); (3) causation (*nexus causalis*) between the amount of damage and the unlawful conduct. At the same time, it cannot be overlooked that fault was previously singled out as one of the separate preconditions for tortious liability. This was justified on the basis that, in the absence of fault, a fortuitous event (*cas*

117. Torgāns, K., Kārkliņš, J. Civiltiesiskās atbildības modeļi pēc vainojamības pazīmes [*Models of Civil Liability by Sign of Fault*]. Jurista Vārds, 2015, Nr.35.
118. Erdmann, C. System des Privatrechts der Ostseeprovinzen Liv-, Est- und Curland. Erster Band. Allgemeiner Theil. Familienrecht. Riga: N. Kymmel's Verlag, 1889, S.261–263.
119. Balodis, K. (2007), *supra* n. 69, 143.lpp.
120. For self-help and self-defence, *see* Sub-Ch.3, Ch.2 of Pt.IV of this monograph *infra*.
121. For consent as a ground of justification, *see* Sub-Ch.1, Ch.2 of Pt.IV of this monograph *infra*.
122. Article 1636 CL.
123. Torgāns, K. (2018) *supra* n. 11, 156.lpp.
124. Judgment of the Supreme Court of 27 Jul. 2020 in Case No. SKC-387/2020 (C29710515), points 7–9.

*fortuit*) or force majeure could be discussed. However, this was not extended to cases where a legal provision provided for no-fault or strict liability.[125] Thus, we should note that in the classic fault-based liability model unlawfulness and fault as requirements for tortious liability should both be analysed, in the context of each other.[126]

*69.* Under Article 1635(1) of the Civil Law, tortious liability may arise only for infringement of a right for which a person may be liable. The equation 'insofar as he may be held at fault' referred to in this provision is essential within the concept of fault liability, which may lead to a person's conduct being recognized as lawful, even though it may seem to an external observer that the person has committed an unlawful act.[127] In this context it seems impossible to speak of an unlawful act if the person acts without intentional or negligent conduct, since such act complies with the prudent and careful (reasonable) person's (*bonus paterfamilias* in Latin) standard.[128] Thus, if no fault is found, an allegation of unlawful conduct itself is incorrect because if there is no fault, there is no unlawfulness.[129] Consequently, a person's conduct, where no fault is established, does not constitute an unlawful act, so that no obligation arises to compensate the victim for the damage caused by this conduct.

*70.* However, unlawfulness should not necessarily be linked to the tortfeasor's fault in the traditional sense of the term. This is particularly evident in the rules of the model of strict liability. Strict liability is discussed separately in Part III of this monograph *infra*; however, it is necessary to outline the concept of strict liability in this sub-chapter from a systematic standpoint. The strict liability model is considered to be an exception, and it is, therefore, necessary to assess, in each case, whether the applicable legal provision excludes fault as a necessary precondition for liability for the damage suffered. Unlike the fault-based liability model, a person within the strict liability model is responsible for infringement of rights, regardless of whether they have committed any lack of care – intent or negligence. This means that, according to the very idea of strict liability, a person cannot rely on the fact of having complied with the necessary due diligence in their activities and that their activities are fully in line with the prudent and careful person's standard (i.e., a reasonable person).[130]

125. Čakste, K. (2011), *supra* n. 69, 192–194.lpp. For strict liability, *see* Pt. III of this monograph *infra*.
126. Buls, L. Vainas nozīme deliktu tiesībās [*Meaning of fault in tort law*]. Grām.: Tiesību efektīvas piemērošanas problemātika. Latvijas Universitātes 72.zinātniskās konferences rakstu krājums [*Problems of Effective Application of Law. The Collection of Writings of the 72th Scientific Conference of the University of Latvia*]. Rīga: LU Akadēmiskais apgāds, 2014, 196.lpp.
127. Torgāns, K., Kārkliņš, J. (2015), *supra* n. 117.
128. *Ibid.*
129. Torgāns, K., Kārkliņš, J., Bitāns, A. (2017), *supra* n. 70, 113.lpp.
130. Torgāns, K., Kārkliņš, J., Bitāns, A. (2017), *supra* n. 70, 297–298.lpp.

§2. CONCEPT OF FAULT: WHAT BEHAVIOUR LEADS TO LIABILITY IN TORT?

*71.* As mentioned in the previous sub-chapter, liability for unlawful acts is dependent on whether the infringer is guilty of fault. Under the general principle envisaged in Latvian tort law, legal responsibility arises for faulty conduct or fault – failure to comply with the standard of diligence required – in the form of negligence (Articles 1644–1646 Civil Law) or intent (Article 1641 Civil Law).[131]

*72.* Thus, *two degrees of fault* are distinguished in Latvian law: wrongful intent and negligence. Meanwhile, negligence is allocated to: (a) gross (*culpa lata*) and (b) ordinary (*culpa levis*). Furthermore, ordinary negligence is allocated to: (a) abstract negligence (*culpa levis in abstracto*) and (b) particular negligence (*culpa levis in concreto* or *diligentia quam in suis*).[132] However, this division of the degrees of negligence in determining tort liability (unlike contractual liability or justifications in strict liability) has no practical significance because in tort law relations the tortfeasor under Article 1649 of the Civil Law is liable for each act of negligence.[133]

*73.* Latvian tort law is familiar with *three models of liability* depending on their relationship with fault – the fault-based liability model, the model of presumption of fault, and the strict liability model, taking the fault-based liability model as general. Note: the absolute liability model does not exist under Latvian tort law.[134]

*74.* The *fault-based liability model* is considered as the general liability model in Latvian tort (and also civil) liability based on Article 1635(1) of the Civil Law discussed above. Under the fault-based liability model, a single or several tortfeasors may be found liable for a tort. In this regard, Article 1650 of the Civil Law regulates liability for mixed fault (*culpa mixta*). Under this provision, when two persons are mutually at fault for negligence, the claims arising therefrom will be mutually adjusted to the extent to which they overlap each other.[135] The abovementioned under Article 1642 of the Civil Law does not, however, apply to cases where both parties have acted in relation to the same subject matter intentionally.

*75.* However, in both modern[136] and historical[137] Latvian legal literature and in recent court practice,[138] considering fault as a precondition for tort liability, it is recognized that a finding of fault is rather linked to a lack of justification. Under this approach, a person who suffers damage must prove that the tortfeasor has committed an unlawful act which was in breach of the law and caused the damage, which

---

131. Kārkliņš, J. Vainas, prettiesiskas rīcības un atbildības ideja privāttiesībās. LU žurnāls 'Juridiskā Zinātne', 8. Sējums [*The Idea of Fault, Illegal Actions and Liability in Private Law. LU Journal 'Juridiskā Zinātne', Volume 8*]. Rīga: Latvijas Universitāte, 2015, 170.lpp.
132. Sinaiskis, V. (1996), *supra* n. 116, 149.lpp.
133. Erdmann, C. (1889), *supra* n. 118, S.266.; Čakste, K. (2011), *supra* n. 69, 195.lpp.
134. Torgāns, K., Kārkliņš, J. (2015), *supra* n. 117.
135. Sinaiskis, V. (1996), *supra* n. 116, 149.lpp.
136. Kubilis, J. (2016), *supra* n. 78, 86–90.lpp.
137. Erdmann, C. (1889), *supra* n. 117, S. 263.
138. Judgment of the Supreme Court of 31 May. 2019 in Case No. SKC-112/2019, point 6.

the tortfeasor can then refute with all the justifications found in the law,[139] for example, by referring to one of the circumstances laid down in Articles 1636 (exercise of subjective right; consent of victim; justified self-defence), 1638 (committing an unlawful act pursuant to the order of a supervisor, if the act is not criminal) and 1733 (self-help) of the Civil Law or by demonstrating compliance of the act or omission with the standard of a prudent and careful (reasonable) person.

*76.* The model of *presumption of fault* may be perceived as a different liability model. In the context of fault as a precondition of tort (and also civil) liability, it is important to note that, under the principle of Latvian tort law, a person is liable for their own 'fault'. Thus, for example, Article 1782 of the Civil Law requires an employer to compensate for damage caused by an employee, while Article 1780 lays down the obligation of parents, guardians, or trustees to compensate damage caused by children (up to the age of seven) or by persons suffering from mental illness. That obligation arises, in the first case, only if the employer is negligent in their selection of employees (*culpa in eligendo*) without verifying their ability and suitability for the post held; and in the second case, if the named persons did not supervise children or mentally ill persons with sufficient care, acting negligently.[140] In both cases, the responsible persons are therefore directly liable for failing to meet the standard of required duty of care regarding their duty to select appropriate employees or to supervise children or persons suffering from mental illness, so that they are liable for their own 'fault'. So it should be concluded that in the above-mentioned cases fault on the part of these subjects is presumed (however, this presumption is rebuttable). At the same time, it would be false to conclude that there is a strict liability model.[141]

*77.* However, liability for quasi-tort is regulated in a twofold way. On the one hand, when determining liability for damage caused by animals[142], a presumption of fault applies, which the keeper of the animal is entitled to rebut.[143] On the other hand, for damage caused by throwing, pouring or falling,[144] the Civil Law imposes liability on the person concerned regardless of fault, thereby setting strict liability.[145]

*78.* Under *the strict liability model*, a person is liable for the consequences even if they have shown the greatest care and fully complied with the standard of a prudent and careful person. The Civil Law also provides such a model of liability in respect of damage caused by a source of abnormal danger; this is regulated in

139. Torgāns, K., Kārkliņš, J. (2015), *supra* n. 117.
140. *Ibid.*
141. For liability of employer for conduct of employees within fulfilment of labour relationships in general, *see* Ch.1 of Pt. II of this monograph *infra*.
142. Article 2363–2368 CL.
143. Torgāns, K., Kārkliņš, J. (2015), *supra* n. 117.
144. Article 2358–2362 CL.
145. Sinaiskis, V. (1996), *supra* n. 116, 234.lpp.

Article 2347(2).[146] It should be noted that the strict liability model also applies under other special laws which will be dealt with in the following chapters.

*79.* Nevertheless, even in the context of strict liability rules, a person still has the possibility to avoid liability by proving the justifications laid down by law, the list of which is generally exhaustive.[147] For example, in relation to liability under Article 2347(2) of the Civil Law for damage caused by a source of abnormal danger, four justifications (force majeure (*vis maior*); gross negligence or intention of the victim; as well as the case where the source of abnormal danger has gone out of the possession of the owner, bailee or user without their fault) are listed which relieve a person of possible tortious liability.[148]

## §3. Duty of Care

*80.* Article 1649 of the Civil Law envisages that the tortfeasor is liable for every act of negligence, even ordinary negligence, in the case of claims arising solely from infringements of a right and which do not affect an existing obligation. Ordinary negligence is the minimum criterion for establishing faulty conduct. Where the required care (in the form of negligence or intent) is lacking, there is fault to be established. This required minimum standard of care is to be found in legal provisions or follows from legal principles or the legal system itself. The yardstick for this standard of care, under Article 1646 of the Civil Law, is the standard of the *prudent and careful person* or conduct expected in accordance with this standard.[149]

*81.* The concept 'prudent and careful person' in Latvian civil law is perceived as the so-called general clause whose content may vary according to time, place and individual circumstances and the assessment of which requires great care not to leave arbitrariness in the hands of the court.[150] As explained in Latvian court practice, the general clause 'prudent and careful person' in the ordinary meaning should be understood as a person who performs their work and duties well and conscientiously, is orderly and precise.[151]

146. Torgāns, K., Kārkliņš, J. (2015), *supra* n. 117.
147. *Ibid.*
148. Bitāns, A. Komentārs Civillikuma 2347.pantam [Commentary of Art. 2347 of the Civil Law]. Grām.: Latvijas Republikas Civillikuma komentāri: Ceturtā daļa. Saistību tiesības [*Commentary to the Civil Law of the Republic of Latvia: Part Four. Law of Obligations*]. (2000), 628–629.lpp.
149. Torgāns, K., Kārkliņš, J., Bitāns, A. (2017), *supra* n. 70, 286–287.lpp.
150. Буковскій, В. Сводъ гражданскихъ узаконеній губерній Прибалтійскихъ съ продолженіемъ 1912–1914 г. г. и съ разъясненіями въ 2 томахъ. Томъ II, содержащій Право требованій [*Compilation of Local Civil Laws of the Baltic Provinces with Continuation 1912–1914. and with Explanations in Two Volumes. Volume 2, Which Contains the Law of Obligations*].Рига: Типографія Г. Гемпель и Ко, 1914, с.1306.
151. Judgment of the Supreme Court of 27 May. 2014 in Case No. SKC-102/2014 (C04326407), point 11.1.

*82.* Consequently, the standard of care tends to vary from one person to another. In the fault-based liability model, negligence is an indispensable prerequisite for tortious liability, while establishing this premise involves, *inter alia,* a person's ability to predict that their conduct will lead to infringement of another person's rights, since failure to predict unforeseeable cases (assessed from the perspective of the average person) in tort law cannot be regarded as negligence.[152]

*83.* Assessing exposure to liability in the fault-based liability model, according to the prediction criterion, involves a three-step test (but not in case of wrongful intent[153]). The first question to be answered is whether the alleged tortfeasor predicted infringement of a right. If the answer is negative, it then has to be decided whether they could subjectively have foreseen an infringement of a right. If the answer is negative, the third question is whether the infringement was objectively foreseeable. A subjective inability to predict infringement of a right does not exonerate an alleged tortfeasor from liability. Objective prediction, on the other hand, is interpreted as a prediction that a prudent and careful person would be able to make.[154] It is important to point out that, in the case of a finding of foreseeable infringement, the ability to predict the extent of damage, unlike contract law,[155] need not and should not be assessed, since the entire amount of damage attributable to a tort must be compensated, even if it was unpredictable.[156]

*84.* It should be noted that the application of the standard of a prudent and careful person and of the predictability test varies, depending on whether the alleged tortfeasor belongs to a particular group of subjects. The law does not impose the same rules of conduct on everyone.[157]

*85.* First, there is the duty of ordinary diligence, which is envisaged in Article 1646 of the Civil Law and applies to every subject of law. Second, there is the duty of diligence, which provides for lower standards of behaviour so that a person's conduct is not found faulty. This group includes specific subjects who are objectively unable to act according to the standard of a prudent and careful person, such as children aged between 7 and 18.[158] Third, there is a standard of increased diligence which provides for higher standards of behaviour so that an individual's conduct cannot be attributed to them. That group includes professionals in a particular field who, objectively, should have a higher level of knowledge and skills in their field than the average member of society, so that the ability to predict the likelihood of

---

152. Torgāns, K., Kārkliņš, J., Bitāns, A. (2017), *supra* n. 70, 292.lpp.
153. Kārkliņš, J. (2015), *supra* n. 117, 164.lpp.
154. Torgāns, K., Kārkliņš, J., Bitāns, A. (2017), *supra* n. 70, 294–295.lpp.; Brants E. *Role of Foreseeability in Imposition of Civil Liability.* In: Socrates: Rīgas Stradiņa niversitates Juridiskās fakultātes elektroniskais juridisko zinātnisko rakstu žurnāls [Rīga Stradiņš University Faculty of Law Electronic Scientific Journal of Law]. Rīga: RSU, 2021, Nr. 2 (20), 269., 272–273., 276., 281.lpp.
155. Art. 1779.[1] CL.
156. Kubilis, J. (2016), *supra* n. 78, 51.lpp.
157. Torgāns, K., Kārkliņš, J., Bitāns, A. (2017), *supra* n. 70, 296. Lpp.; Brants E. Bezdarbība kā vainojamas rīcības izpausme deliktu tiesībās [*Omission as an Expression of Fault in Tort Law*]. Jurista Vārds, 2021, Nr.25/26, 47.lpp.
158. Torgāns, K., Kārkliņš, J., Bitāns, A. (2017), *supra* n. 70, 297.lpp.

infringement of rights must also be higher. An example of such a specific person is a merchant who is required by law[159] to comply with the specific diligence of a merchant. Similarly, members of a company's board and council, doctors, lawyers, engineers, builders, and the like, are obliged to obey a standard of increased diligence.[160]

## §4. Capacity: Infants and Minors

*86.* Under Latvian tort law,[161] children under the age of 7 as well as persons with mental or other health disorders, who are not able to understand the meaning of their actions or are not able to control their actions, are not responsible for any damage they cause to another person. Likewise, a person with the capacity to act will not be held liable in tort if they committed the tort while unconscious or unable to understand the meaning of their action or unable to control their action. However, a person whose condition is self-induced by means of alcohol or other means will be held liable in tort. As regards the last sentence, we should note the difference from contract law,[162] under which a legal transaction is void where a person has led to them being unconscious or otherwise in a condition of being unable to understand.[163] But certainly, not all of the effects of drunkenness or other confusion of consciousness amount to a temporary lessening of capacity, since normally, alcohol can lead to lethargic, reckless or other aberrant behaviour, which does not, however, exclude the existence of will in a transaction.[164]

*87.* As mentioned previously, the victim of a tort committed by a person not responsible for their actions under Article 1780 of the Civil Law may nevertheless have a claim against the parents, guardians, or trustee of a tortfeasor. Under Article 1780 of the Civil Law, a person whose duty it is to supervise persons of reduced capacity is bound to compensate for any damage caused through unlawful action by those persons. The duty to compensate does not arise if the supervisor can prove that they fulfilled their duty to supervise with the diligence of a prudent and careful person.[165] Meanwhile, if the supervisor has not admitted negligence or does not have any property capable of compensating for damage, the damage will be compensated from the property of the tortfeasor to the extent that they are not deprived

159. Article 393(1) KCL.
160. Torgāns, K., Kārkliņš, J., Bitāns, A. (2017), *supra* n. 70, 297.lpp.; Novicāne E. Valdes locekļa atbildība par kapitālsabiedrībai nodarītajiem zaudējumiem [*Liability of a Member of the Board for Damages Caused to the Capital Company*]. Rīga: Tiesu namu aģentūra, 2021, 39–40.lpp.
161. Article 1637 CL.
162. Article 1409 CL.
163. Balodis, K. (2007), *supra* n. 69, 79.lpp.
164. Torgāns K. Komentārs Civillikuma 1409.pantam [Commentary to Article 1409 of Civil Law]. Grām.: Latvijas Republikas Civillikuma komentāri: Ceturtā daļa. Saistību tiesības [*Commentary to the Civil Law of the Republic of Latvia: Part Four. Law of Obligations*]. (2000), 24–25.lpp.
165. Буковскій, В. (1914), *supra* n. 150, c.1402.

of the means needed for their maintenance.[166] Thus, there is no strict liability for employers, guardians or parents in Latvian tort law (in this regard *see* further in Part II Chapters 1 and 2).

166. Torgāns, K. Komentārs Civillikuma 1780.pantam [*Commentary of Article 1780 of Civil Law*]. Grām.: Latvijas Republikas Civillikuma komentāri: Ceturtā daļa. Saistību tiesības [*Commentary to the Civil Law of the Republic of Latvia: Part Four. Law of Obligations*]. (2000), 273.lpp.

# Chapter 2. Specific Cases of Liability: Are All Tortfeasors Subject to the Same Rules?

## §1. LIABILITY OF PROFESSIONALS

### I. In General: Is There a Higher Standard of Care?

*88.* As noted previously, many professionals, such as merchants, medical practitioners, advocates, company board and council members, engineers, builders, and the like, have a higher standard of care.[167] This is not, however, established as a general rule in a single legal act. Instead, the increased higher standard of care can be deduced from the legal system as a whole, as well as many special legal acts regulating the activities of each profession.

### II. Medical Practitioners

*89.* The Law on the Rights of Patients regulates a special procedure by which a patient can realize the right to compensation for non-pecuniary damage caused to their life or health by the conduct of medical practitioners working in a medical institution or conditions during medical treatment. The particular legal act also presupposes a patient's right to compensation for expenses related to medical treatment if medical treatment had been necessary to eliminate or reduce the unfavourable consequences of damage to the life or health of the patient caused by a medical practitioner or conditions during medical treatment.[168]

*90.* Patients' rights to compensation for non-pecuniary damage caused by medical practitioners or conditions during medical treatment since 25 October 2016 are generally exploited within administrative rather than civil proceedings. This is due to the fact that since this date,[169] similarly to Sweden and Denmark,[170] compensation for such damage is generally paid from the Medical Treatment Risk Fund. As noted by the Supreme Court, the Medical Treatment Risk Fund was set up to make it easier for a patient to receive compensation.[171] This is done, among other things, through administrative proceedings. In contrast to civil proceedings, where the adversarial principle prevails and each party has to prove to the court the merits of

167. *See* Ch. 1 of Pt. I of this monograph *supra*.
168. Article 16(1) Law on the Rights of Patients. Official translation into English available on the official web-page of the State Language Centre at https://vvc.gov.lv/image/catalog/dokumenti/Law%20on%20the%20Rights%20of%20Patients.docx [accessed on 28 Feb. 2022].
169. Transitional provision No.1 of the Law on the Rights of Patients, *supra* n. 168; *see also* Brikmane E. Darbību uzsāk Ārstniecības riska fonds [*The Medical Risk Fund has been Launched*]. LV portals. Available in Latvian at https://lvportals.lv/skaidrojumi/259330-darbibu-uzsak-arstniecibas-riska-fonds-2013 [accessed on 30 Aug. 2021.]
170. Judgment of the Supreme Court of 26 Jun. 2019 in Case No. SKA-453/2019 (A420300316), point 11.
171. *Ibid.*, point 8.

its claims, counterclaims, and objections,[172] in administrative proceedings, one of the basic principles is the principle of objective investigation.[173] The institutions and the administrative court under the principle of objective investigation have an obligation to give instructions and recommendations to the participants in the proceedings, including the patient, as well as to collect proof on their own initiative.[174]

*91.* Payment of compensation from the Medical Treatment Risk Fund in administrative proceedings does not preclude the possibility of establishing a medical practitioner's or a medical institution's liability in civil proceedings. The legal literature has acknowledged that this can be in situations where the Law on the Rights of Patients does not presuppose rights to compensation for particular damage or if compensation from the Medical Treatment Risk Fund does not fully compensate for damage caused.[175] This has also been confirmed by the Latvian Constitutional Court, which has stated that:

> Damage caused to the life or health of a patient caused by the conditions or the conduct of a medical practitioner in the course of treatment can also cause damage to other persons, which must be compensated in civil proceedings. For example, a patient's relatives may experience mental suffering due to damage to a patient's health or death of the patient. In the event of a patient's death, their relatives may also suffer pecuniary damage, such as funeral expenses. In addition, it is possible that the patient's medical expenses were covered by the patient's relative or another person.[176]

---

172. Rozenbergs, J., Torgāns, K. Komentārs Civilprocesa likuma 10.pantam [*Commentary of Article 10 of the Civil Procedure Law*]. Grām.: Civilprocesa likuma komentāri. I daļa (1–28.nodaļa). Otrais papildinātais izdevums [*Commentary to the Civil Procedure Law. Part I (Chapters 1 to 28). Second supplemented edition*]. Sagatavojis autoru kolektīvs. Prof. K.Torgāna zinātniskajā redakcijā. Rīga: Tiesu namu aģentūra, 2016, 62.lpp.
173. Autoru kolektīvs. Administratīvais process tiesā [*Administrative Proceedings in Court*]. Dr.iur. J. Briedes vispārīgā zinātniskā redakcijā. Rīga: Latvijas Vēstnesis, 2008, 260–261.lpp.
174. Article 107(1) Administrative Procedure Law. Official translation into English available on the official web-page of the State Language Centre at https://vvc.gov.lv/image/catalog/dokumenti/Administrative%20Procedure%20Law.docx [accessed on 28 Feb. 2022]. Although the relevant legal norm textually presupposes the principle of objective investigation only for the administrative courts, court practice has recognized that this principle equally applies to institutions. *See* in this regard Augstākās Tiesas prakses vispārinājums 'Objektīvās izmeklēšanas princips – interpretācija un piemērošana' [*Generalization of the Supreme Court court practice 'Principle of Objective Investigation – Interpretation and Application'*], 27–28.lpp. Available in Latvian at https://at.gov.lv/files/uploads/files/6_Judikatura/Tiesu_prakses_apkopojumi/2016/1-Obj_izm_princips_visparinajums-2005.doc [accessed on 3 Sep. 2021.].
175. Rožkalns, R. Komentārs Pacientu tiesību likuma 16.pantam [*Commentary to Article 16 of the Law on the Rights of Patients*]. Grām.: Pacientu tiesību likuma komentāri [*Commentary to the Law on the Rights of Patients*]. LL.D. S. Slokenbergas zinātniskā redakcijā. Rīga: Latvijas Vēstnesis, 2019, 286–287.lpp. In this regard, it must be noted that the Law on the Rights of Patients limits the amount of compensation to be paid to patients. Under Art. 16(2)(1) of the Law on the Rights of Patients a patient has the right to receive compensation from the Medical Treatment Risk Fund for harm caused to their life or health in the amount of the harm caused, but not more than 142,290 EUR. Under Art. 16(2)($2^1$) medical expenses are compensated in the amount of the expenses incurred, but not more than 28,460 EUR.
176. Judgment of the Constitutional Court of 18 Oct. 2018 in Case No. 2017-33-03, point 15.1.

*92.* The legal literature has recognized that the patient has a right to claim compensation under the Law on the Rights of Patients not only for physical damage (such as bodily injuries caused by poor quality surgery) but also if medical treatment was performed without the informed consent of the patient, if information about the patient was unlawfully disclosed, as well as in other cases.[177] It must be emphasized that Article 16(1) of the Law on the Rights of Patients also presupposes compensation for damage caused by conditions during medical treatment, distinguishing this from damaging conduct by a medical practitioner. Within the meaning of this provision, conditions during medical treatment can be considered, such as conditions in a medical institution, conditions during the patient's transportation, and the like, which have caused damage to the patient's health or life.[178]

*93.* Payment of compensation from the Medical Treatment Risk Fund is not related to the medical practitioner's fault in causing damage to the patient, i.e., the patient is entitled to compensation under the Law on the Rights of Patients for damage caused even if the medical practitioner has done everything in good conscience and no medical practitioner's fault can be established.[179] This does not, however, mean that medical practitioners are held liable under the strict liability model. Compensation for damage regardless of fault on the part of their medical practitioner does not mean that the patient must be compensated for all unfavourable medical treatment.[180] The unavoidable consequences of well-chosen treatment and adverse reactions and complications beyond the control of the medical practitioner are not considered as damage to be compensated. Thus, although payment of compensation from the Medical Treatment Risk Fund is not related to fault on the part of the medical practitioner, it is payable only if unprofessional conduct by the medical practitioner or inappropriate conditions during medical treatment are established.[181] In this regard, it has been noted that a patient is entitled to compensation for the damage that an experienced specialist could have prevented.[182] The conduct of the medical practitioner can be assessed in the light of clinical guidelines, the latest scientific studies and opinions, as well as the opinions of professional organizations of medical practitioners, individual experts, and other sources.[183]

*94.* In cases concerning a patient's right to compensation from the Medical Treatment Risk Fund, the 'probability predominance' standard of proof is used to establish a causal link. This standard does not require that all reasonable doubts as to the existence of a causal link be ruled out. Instead, it must be established that the

177. Rožkalns, R. (2019), *supra* n. 175, 273–274.lpp.
178. Decision on the action, sitting of the Supreme Court of 17 Jun. 2021 in Case No. SKA-198/2021 (A420162118), point 6.
179. Judgment of the Supreme Court of 26 Jun. 2019 in Case No. SKA-453/2019 (A420300316), point 11.
180. Rožkalns, R. (2019), *supra* n. 175, 284.lpp.
181. Judgment of the Supreme Court of 24 Mar. 2020 in Case No. SKA-79/2020 (A420172018), point 9.
182. Judgment of the Supreme Court of 26 Jun. 2019 in Case No. SKA-453/2019 (A420300316), point 11.
183. Judgment of the Supreme Court of 20 Nov. 2020 in Case No. SKA-1002/2020 (A420192617), point 8.

likelihood that a causal link exists is greater than the likelihood that it does not exist.[184] Furthermore, if, even after all the evidence has been obtained, it cannot be clearly concluded that the likelihood of a causal link is greater than the likelihood that it does not exist (i.e., the existence of a causal link is as likely as the absence of one), a conclusion regarding the causal link must be drawn in favour of the patient.[185]

*95.* Another noteworthy aspect regarding compensation for damage to a person's health presupposed by the Law on the Rights of Patients can be observed in the context of inheritance law. Although principally, the right to compensation for damage to a person's health is by nature purely personal and therefore cannot be inherited,[186] the Latvian Constitutional Court has recognized that:

> Article 16(1) of the Law on the Rights of Patients provides for an exception to the general legal order according to which the right of claim of a purely personal nature cannot be inherited. Pursuant to this provision, in the event of a patient's death, the right to receive compensation from the Medical Treatment Risk Fund for non-pecuniary damage caused to him becomes part of the patient's inheritance.[187]

## III. Legal Practitioners

*96.* The liability of advocates is regulated by Latvia's Advocacy Law.[188] Article 110 of the Advocacy Law provides that:

> The client has the right to claim damages from the advocate who provided him with legal assistance. An unfavourable outcome of the case for the client or another unfavourable result of the provision of legal assistance shall not be the basis for the liability of an advocate if all the grounds for liability have not been established.

---

184. Judgment of the Supreme Court of 26 Jun. 2019 in Case No. SKA-453/2019 (A420300316), point 11.; Judgment of the Supreme Court of 12 Apr. 2021 in Case No. SKA-156/2021 (A420217416), point 8.
185. Senāta prakses apkopojums 'Par atlīdzību no Ārstniecības riska fonda. Senāta judikatūras atziņas (2015–2021.gada jūlijs)' [*Summary of Senate practice 'For Remuneration from the Medical Treatment Risk Fund. Findings of the Settled Court Practice of the Senate (July 2015–2021)*], 10.lpp. Available in Latvian at https://www.at.gov.lv/files/uploads/files/6_Judikatura/Tiesu_prakses_apkopojumi/2021/Arstniecibas_riska_fonds_Senata_atzinas.docx [accessed on 6 Sep. 2021.].
186. Gencs, Z., Krauze, R. Komentārs Civillikuma 704.pantam [*Commentary to Article 704 of the Civil Law*]. Grām.: Civillikuma komentāri: Mantojuma tiesības [*Commentary to the Civil Law. Inheritance Law*]. Rīga: Mans Īpašums, 1997, 267.lpp.
187. Judgment of the Constitutional Court of 18 Oc. 2018 in Case No. 2017-33-03, point 15.3.
188. Article 70 Advocacy Law of the Republic of Latvia. Official translation into English available on the official web-page of the State Language Centre at https://vvc.gov.lv/image/catalog/dokumenti/Advocacy%20Law%20of%20the%20Republic%20of%20Latvia.doc [accessed on 17 Jan. 2022].

Thus, an unfavourable result by itself is not sufficient to establish the liability of an advocate. It is necessary to establish an infringement of professional activity committed by the advocate, as well as a causal link between the infringement and the damage caused.[189]

*97.* As noted previously, advocates operate under a higher standard of care.[190] A higher standard of care is presupposed due to the special status of advocates. Advocacy is established as a system within which strict requirements are set for the admission of new members[191] and in which a control mechanism functions, monitoring the professional activities of advocates, their observance of ethical requirements, as well as maintaining and improving their qualification. In addition, advocates are the only legal advisers who belong to the court system, giving them wider powers and opportunities to defend the client's interests. This guarantees the efficiency and quality of the legal aid provided by an advocate.[192] Thus, the Latvian Constitutional Court has recognized that the ability of advocates to provide qualified legal representation and legal aid is presumed, considering their status.[193] Similar conclusions have also been expressed in the court practice of the Supreme Court.[194]

*98.* In addition to personal liability, sworn advocates under Article 111 of the Latvian Advocacy Law are liable for the activities of assistants to sworn advocates. Sworn advocates and offices of sworn advocates under Article 118 of Latvia's Advocacy Law can also be held liable for the activities of employed technical, financial, or advisory staff who are prohibited from providing legal assistance. Under Article 114 of Latvia's Advocacy Law, potential damages caused by the professional activities of advocates must be insured.

## IV. Builders and Architects

*99.* Liability in the construction sector is based on the general principle of civil law according to which each construction specialist and participant in the construction process is obliged to compensate other participants in the construction process and third persons for damage caused by their faulty actions or omissions.[195] This is

189. Novicāne, E. Pārvaldība un atbildība pēc zvērinātu advokātu biroju tiesiskā statusa reformas [*Governance and Responsibility Following Reform of the Legal Status of the Offices of Sworn Advocates*]. Jurista Vārds, 2021, Nr.10.
190. Torgāns, K., Kārkliņš, J., Bitāns, A. (2017), *supra* n. 70, 297.lpp.
191. The legal framework presupposes many requirements for this profession: higher legal education, work experience, the need to pass examinations, etc.; *see* Judgment of the Constitutional Court of 27 Jun. 2003 in Case No. 2003-04-01, point 4.1. of the concluding part.
192. Decision of the Constitutional Court of 6 Apr. 2017 on termination of legal proceedings in Case No. 2016-10-01, point 16.
193. Judgment of the Constitutional Court of 27 Jun. 2003 in Case No. 2003-04-01, point 4.1. of the concluding part.
194. Judgment of the Supreme Court of 31 Oct. 2019 in Case No. SKC-316/2019 (C33431717), point 7.
195. Article 1635 CL.

generally done in accordance with the procedure specified in the Construction Law and the Civil Law,[196] though, in addition to these legal acts, some aspects of the liability of construction specialists (such as their professional duties[197]) are regulated in general and special construction regulations.

*100.* The Construction Law distinguishes the professional liability of construction specialists[198] as natural persons from the liability of participants in the construction process which can be either natural or legal entities (construction merchants). Further, the Construction Law separates the liability of each participant in the construction process, i.e., each participant is liable for its part of the construction process.[199] In this regard, the Construction Law sets apart six participants in the construction process: (1) the initiator of the construction, (2) the developer of the construction design, (3) the performer of construction works, (4) the performer of author's supervision, (5) the performer of construction supervision, and (6) the performer of construction inspection.[200] The liability and the general obligations of each above-mentioned participant in the construction process are regulated in Articles 19 to 19.[3] of the Construction Law.

*101.* The Construction Law also specifies the persons who are liable for eliminating the consequences of unauthorized construction. Generally, the persons who are liable for unauthorized construction under Article 19(3) of the Construction Law are the owners of the plot of land and, if construction works have been performed on a structure, the owners of the structure. This corresponds to the general principle presupposed in the Civil Law and legal acts regulating the construction process that the owner of an immovable property is deemed to be a person who has the exclusive power to decide on the use, maintenance, and, accordingly, construction on their property. In turn, in addition to the rights of the owner of immovable property, there is also an obligation to be liable for compliance with the requirements of legal norms regulating the use (including construction) of the property.[201] However, in specific cases of unauthorized construction, the persons who can be held liable for eliminating the consequences include the legal possessor of the plot of land, the

196. Likumprojekta 'Grozījumi Būvniecības likumā' sākotnējās ietekmes novērtējuma ziņojums (anotācija) [*Initial impact assessment report on 'Amendments to the Construction Law' bill (annotation)*]. Available: http://titania.saeima.lv/LIVS13/SaeimaLIVS13.nsf/0/B723945BD75B42CCC22585040051B820?OpenDocument [accessed on 30 Aug. 2021.].

197. Article 19.[3] (1) Construction Law. Official translation into English available on the official webpage of the State Language Centre at https://vvc.gov.lv/image/catalog/dokumenti/Construction%20Law.docx [accessed on 17 Jan. 2022]

198. As stated in Art. 13(1) of the Construction Law, *supra* n. 197: *'Construction specialists are persons who have acquired the right to an independent practice in the field of architecture, construction, or electric energy in regulated professions.'*

199. Likumprojekta 'Grozījumi Būvniecības likumā' sākotnējās ietekmes novērtējuma ziņojums (anotācija) [*Initial impact assessment report of the 'Amendments to the Construction Law' bill (annotation)*]. Available: http://titania.saeima.lv/LIVS13/SaeimaLIVS13.nsf/0/B723945BD75B42CCC22585040051B820?OpenDocument [accessed on 30 Aug. 2021.].

200. Article 1(15) Construction Law, *supra* n. 197.

201. Judgment of the Supreme Court of 26 Apr. 2019 in Case No. SKA-262/2019 (A420139316), point 9.

legal possessor of the structure, the superficiary (a person who has built on the soil of another by agreement), and the initiator of the construction.[202]

*102.* Since each participant in the construction process has their own liability, professional duties, and competence within the construction process,[203] Article 19(1) of the Construction Law presupposes that the approvals provided by the participants in the construction process within the process do not release other participants in the construction process from liability.[204]

*103.* Construction specialists (except those who are obliged to supervise or inspect work performed by another construction specialist or its result), while performing the duties specified in legal acts, are entitled to assume that other construction specialists involved in implementing the construction plan are acting in accordance with legal acts and are performing their professional duties qualitatively. However, a construction specialist who, in accordance with their professional knowledge and experience, finds obvious violations of the requirements of legal acts in the professional activities of another construction specialist must act in such a way as to prevent damage to life, health, property or the environment.[205]

*104.* The Construction Law provides two types of compulsory insurance of civil liability. First, under Article 13(10) of the Construction Law, construction specialists are obliged to insure their professional liability for damage to the life, health, property of other construction participants and third persons, as well as to the environment caused by their acts or omissions during the construction process. In this case, the liability of the construction specialist as a natural person is insured, i.e., liability for damage caused as a result of professional activity. Second, Article 20(1) of the Construction Law presupposes that a builder (or, as used in the Construction Law, performer of construction works) has an obligation to insure their civil liability. In this case, the civil liability of the builder (which can be either a natural person or a construction merchant) is insured against damage caused to third persons during and as a result of the construction works.

*105.* It must be noted that Article 2347(2) of the Civil Law indicates construction, among other things, as a source of abnormal danger and thus presupposes compensation of damage caused in the construction process under the strict liability model. Although no extensive court practice has been developed in the application of this legal norm, it has been recognized in the legal literature that Article 2347(2) of the Civil Law should be viewed in the light of the fact that not every construction process is associated with increased risk to others.[206]

202. Article 19(3) Construction Law, *supra* n. 197.
203. Likumprojekta 'Grozījumi Būvniecības likumā' sākotnējās ietekmes novērtējuma ziņojums (anotācija) [*Initial impact assessment report on 'Amendments to the Construction Law' bill (annotation)*], *supra* n. 196.
204. Article 19(1) Construction Law, *supra* n. 197.
205. Article 19.[3] (2) Construction Law, *supra* n. 197.
206. Kubilis, J. (2016), *supra* n. 78, 225.lpp.

## V. Others

*106.* Both the Latvian Constitutional Court[207] and Supreme Court[208] have noted that a merchant's standard of care must be distinguished from the standard of an average natural person. This is envisaged in Article 393(1) of the Commercial Law (KCL), which presupposes a specific standard of care for merchants by providing that they must act with the diligence of a prudent and accurate merchant. Even though this provision textually presupposes a merchant's higher standard of care in relations involving commercial transactions and thus concerns only contractual liability, the merchant's higher standard of care equally applies to tortious liability since merchants in their relevant field should objectively have a higher level of knowledge and skill than the average natural person.

*107.* The KCL also provides special regulation of the liability of board and council members. Article 169(1) of the KCL states that members of the board and the council must perform their obligations as would a prudent and careful person. In addition, under Article 169(2) of the KCL, board and council members are solidarily (i.e., jointly and severally) liable for damage that they cause the company. The scope of this provision, however, only regulates the liability of board and council members against a commercial company. The provision does not affect the tortious liability of board and council members against third persons, which is established on the general grounds presupposed in the Civil Law.[209]

*108.* Although textually, Article 169(1) of the KCL corresponds to the general standard of care laid down in Article 1646 of the Civil Law by imposing on board and council members a duty to act as a reasonable person (a prudent and careful person), Latvian legal doctrine[210] and court practice have recognized that the KCL presupposes a higher standard of care than the Civil Law where a commercial company is concerned. In this regard, the Supreme Court has noted that:

> The provisions of the Civil Law on tort liability may be applied against members of the board of a company for damage caused to a third person by tortious conduct, but in relations with the company the Commercial Law imposes stricter requirements on a board member.[211]

*109.* Liability of board and council members against commercial companies occurs, if (1) the company has suffered damage, (2) there has been conduct by a board or council member, and (3) there is a causal link between the conduct of the

---

207. Judgment of the Constitutional Court of 8 Mar. 2017 in Case No. 2016-07-01, point 24.1.
208. Judgment of the Supreme Court of 25 Nov. 2020 in Case No. SKC-41/2020 (C28330013), point 10.5.
209. Strupišs, A. Komentārs Komerclikuma 169.pantam [*Commentary to Article 169 of the Commercial Law*], 2019. Available at https://komentari.info/index.php?lv=1&likums=4&komentars=170 [accessed on 30 Aug. 2021.]
210. Novicāne, E. (2021), *supra* n. 160, 39–40.lpp.
211. Judgment of the Supreme Court of 25 Jan. 2012 in Case No. SKC-25/2012, point 8.4.

board or council member and the damage suffered by the company.[212] The Supreme Court has recognized that a commercial company must first prove the existence of damage and the fact that this has arisen due to the conduct of a member of the management board or council. It is not for a commercial company, however, to prove that a board or council member acted with fault.[213] Such a procedure derogates from the general principle of civil procedure regarding the burden of proof,[214] since the member of the board or council must rebut the presumption of unlawfulness and fault in terms of their conduct. Liability does not arise only if a board or council member proves that they acted as a prudent and careful person in the relevant situation, i.e., that they did not act even with ordinary negligence.[215] In a situation where a board or council member is not able to prove that, their fault is presumed.[216]

*110.* Outside the legal framework of the KCL, several other legal acts regulate compulsory insurance for the professional civil liability of specific professions. In addition to advocates[217] and construction specialists,[218] among others, notaries,[219] bailiffs,[220] insolvency administrators,[221] and outsourced accountants[222] must insure against their professional civil liability.

212. Strupišs, A., *supra* n. 209.
213. Judgment of the Supreme Court of 30 Nov. 2017 in Case No. SKC-343/2017, point 9.1.
214. Judgment of the Supreme Court of 29 Dec. 2017 in Case No. SKC-351/2017 (C04254513), point 7.1.
215. Article 169(3) Commercial Law. Official translation into English available on the official web-page of the State Language Centre at https://vvc.gov.lv/image/catalog/dokumenti/Commercial%20Law.docx [accessed on 28 Feb. 2022.].; Judgment of the Supreme Court of 13 Mar. 2020 in Case No. SKC-122/2020 (C29378917), point 7.2.; Judgment of the Supreme Court of 7 Jun. 2016 in Case No. SKC-7/2016 (C39072411), point 7.4.
216. Decision in the action, sitting of the Supreme Court of 28 Apr. 2020 in Case No. SKC-208/2020 (C30601515), point 2.1.; Judgment of the Supreme Court of 7 Jun. 2016 in Case No. SKC-7/2016 (C39072411), point 7.4.
217. *See* Pt I. Liability for One's Own Acts, Chapter 2. Specific Cases of Liability, §1. Liability of Professionals, III. Legal Practitioners.
218. *See* Pt I. Liability for One's Own Acts, Chapter 2. Specific Cases of Liability, §1. Liability of Professionals, IV. Builders and Architects.
219. Articles 24–30 Notariate Law. Official translation into English available on the official web-page of the State Language Centre at https://vvc.gov.lv/image/catalog/dokumenti/Notariate%20Law.docx [accessed on 17 Jan. 2022].
220. Arts 33–39 Law on Bailiffs. Official translation into English available on the official web-page of the State Language Centre at https://vvc.gov.lv/image/catalog/dokumenti/Law%20on%20Bailiffs.docx [accessed on 17 Jan. 2022].
221. Article 31 Insolvency Law. Official translation into English available on the official web-page of the State Language Centre at https://vvc.gov.lv/image/catalog/dokumenti/Insolvency%20Law.docx [accessed on 17 Jan. 2022].
222. Article 3.[1] Law on Accounting. Official translation into English available on the official web-page of the State Language Centre at https://vvc.gov.lv/image/catalog/dokumenti/Accounting%20Law.docx [accessed on 17 Jan. 2022].

§2. Liability of Public Authorities

*111.* 108. Under the third sentence of Article 92 of the *Satversme*, everyone has a fundamental right to compensation for damage caused by public authorities. The liability of public authorities can be established under either the Civil Law or one of several other legal acts. This depends on whether the public authority has caused damage to an individual as a result of conduct in the private sphere or the public sphere, i.e., what has to be assessed is whether the conduct can be carried out only by an entity endowed with public authority.[223]

*112.* The concept of civil liability is used in the field of Administrative Law, i.e., liability for an infringement of Administrative Law established in administrative proceedings.[224] In administrative, legal relations, the right to compensation for damage caused by public authorities is presupposed in Article 92 of the Administrative Procedure Law, while the realization of this right is regulated in more detail in the Law on Compensation for Damage Caused by State Administrative Institutions.[225]

*113.* Generally, a state administrative institution may cause damage by actions, i.e., by issuing an unlawful administrative act or by performing an actual unlawful action, or by omissions, if the authority was obliged to act but has unlawfully not acted.[226] The Supreme Court has also recognized that:

> The *Satversme* calls for consideration to be given to the need for compensation also in cases where the damage is the result of a lawful administrative act or actual action, i.e., in certain cases, in the interests of justice, it must be decided to compensate a person even if the public administration's conduct complies with legal norms and no unlawfulness can be ascertained.[227]

However, not all restrictions of rights arising from the legal conduct of a state institution have to be compensated. What must be assessed is whether there is a restriction of a person's rights that causes them to suffer different, special, and extraordinary damage when compared to others.[228]

223. Briede, J., Danovskis, E., Kovaļevska, A. (2021), *supra* n. 49, 25–26.lpp.
224. Torgāns, K. (2018), *supra* n. 11, 487.lpp.
225. Judgment of the Supreme Court of 5 Apr. 2011 in Case No. SKA-25/2011 (A42440505), point 10.; Judgment of the Supreme Court of 16 Feb. 2010 in Case No. SKA-104/2010 (A42466905), point 11.
226. Article 4(1) Law on Compensation for Damages Caused by State Administrative Institutions. No English translation is available.
227. Judgment of the Supreme Court of 24 Sep. 2019 in Case No. SKA-1528/2019 (A670010319), point 10.
228. *Ibid.*, point 12.

*114.* Persons entitled to compensation are individuals who are addressees of an administrative act or third persons within the meaning of the Administrative Procedure Law, as well as individuals directly affected by the actual action of the institution.[229] A relative of a natural person who has died as a result of conduct by a public authority may also be a victim entitled to compensation.[230]

*115.* To ensure that the state is liable only for damage resulting from a mistake by a public authority and not damage suffered by an individual regardless of the conduct of a public authority,[231] the right to compensation arises if there is a direct causal link between conduct by the institution and damage suffered by the victim.[232] Thus, the need arises to distinguish damage that is not directly caused by an administrative act of (or actual action by) a public authority or whose connection with the administrative act (or actual action) is remote.[233] There is no causal link where the same damage would have occurred if the institution had acted lawfully.[234]

*116.* Both pecuniary and non-pecuniary damage are compensated under the Law on Compensation for Damage Caused by State Administrative Institutions.[235] In cases of substantial infringement of rights caused to an individual by an administrative act or actual action, the existence of non-pecuniary damage is deemed to be proved.[236]

*117.* The amount of compensation to be paid is calculated by taking into account both the conduct of the state administrative institution and the victim.[237] The victim is not entitled to compensation if they have not done everything possible to prevent or reduce the damage, using their knowledge, abilities, and practical possibilities.[238]

229. Article 5(1) Law on Compensation for Damages Caused by State Administrative Institutions, *supra* n. 226.
230. Article 5(2) Law on Compensation for Damages Caused by State Administrative Institutions, *supra* n. 226.
231. Judgment of the Supreme Court of 28 Oct. 2019 in Case No. SKA-200/2019 (A420312014), point 5.
232. Article 6(1) Law on Compensation for Damages Caused by State Administrative Institutions, *supra* n. 226.
233. Judgment of the Supreme Court of 6 Dec. 2017 in Case No. SKA-302/2017 (A420500912), point 9.
234. Article 6(2) Law on Compensation for Damages Caused by State Administrative Institutions, *supra* n. 226.
235. Articles 7–8 Law on Compensation for Damages Caused by State Administrative Institutions, *supra* n. 226.
236. Article 11(3) Law on Compensation for Damages Caused by State Administrative Institutions, *supra* n. 226.
237. Articles 12–13 Law on Compensation for Damages Caused by State Administrative Institutions, *supra* n. 226.
238. Article 10(1) Law on Compensation for Damages Caused by State Administrative Institutions, *supra* n. 226.

A victim is also not entitled to receive compensation for damage if they have facilitated the occurrence or increase of the amount of damage caused.[239] In addition, the Law on Compensation for Damage Caused by State Administrative Institutions limits the amount of pecuniary[240] and non-pecuniary damage[241] to be compensated.

*118.* The legal framework presupposed in the Law on Compensation for Damages Caused by State Administrative Institutions allows compensation in kind. A state institution may, at its discretion, compensate both pecuniary and non-pecuniary damage caused to a victim in such a way that instead of paying monetary compensation, the victim's previous situation is restored (restitution).[242] In cases of non-pecuniary damage, an apology may also be an acceptable remedy for the damage caused.[243]

*119.* The liability of public authorities is not, however, only regulated in the sphere of administrative law. A tort may also be manifest in the conduct of persons in the service of judicial institutions – for example, by performing investigative actions, applying security measures, applying compulsory measures of a medical nature, suspending a person from their position – which is later recognized as unlawful or unreasonable conduct.[244] The legal basis for the material liability of these institutions is established in the Law on Compensation for Damage Caused in Criminal Proceedings and Administrative Infringement Record-Keeping. In addition, the liability of public authorities in specific sectors is regulated in several other legal acts. For example, the Credit Institution Law regulates the liability of the national financial regulatory authority, the Financial and Capital Market Commission,[245] while the Law on Prevention of Money Laundering and Terrorism and Proliferation Financing details the liability of Latvia's Financial Intelligence Unit.[246]

---

239. Article 10(2) Law on Compensation for Damages Caused by State Administrative Institutions, *supra* n. 226.
240. Under Art. 13(3) of the Law on Compensation for Damage Caused by State Administrative Institutions, *supra* n. 226, damages are normally compensated in the following amount: if damages exceed 145,000 EUR – 100% of this amount; if the damages exceed 145,000 EUR, but do not exceed 1,450,000 EUR – 145,000 EUR plus 50 to 100% of the amount exceeding 145,000 EUR; and if the damages exceed 1,450,000 EUR, appropriate compensation can be less than 50% of this amount.
241. Under Art. 14(4) of the Law on Compensation for Damages Caused by State Administrative Institutions, *supra* n. 226, the general limit for compensation for non-pecuniary damage is 7,000 EUR. In the event of serious non-pecuniary damage, compensation can be up to 10,000 EUR, but in the case of harm to life or particularly serious harm to health – up to 30,000 EUR.
242. Articles 13(4) and 14(2) of the Law on Compensation for Damages Caused by State Administrative Institutions, *supra* n. 226.
243. Article 14(2) Law on Compensation for Damages Caused by State Administrative Institutions, *supra* n. 226.
244. Torgāns, K. (2018), *supra* n. 11, 489.lpp.
245. *See* Art. 111 Credit Institution Law. Official translation into English available on the official web-page of the State Language Centre at https://vvc.gov.lv/image/catalog/dokumenti/Credit%20Institution%20Law.docx [accessed on 17 Jan. 2022].
246. *See* Ch. XIV Law on the Prevention of Money Laundering and Terrorism and Proliferation Financing. Official translation into English available on the official web-page of the State Language Centre at https://vvc.gov.lv/image/catalog/dokumenti/Law%20on%20the%20Prevention%20of%20Money%20Laundering%20and%20Terrorism%20Financing.docx [accessed on 17 Jan.2022].

## §3. Abuse of Rights

*120.* Under Article 1 of the Civil Law, the principle of good faith must be taken into account by civil law subjects in the exercise of legal rights. It is generally accepted that, under the principle of good faith, right-holders must take into account the legitimate interests of others when exercising their rights and performing their duties.[247] The principle of good faith is based on the recognition that in exercising their rights and performing their duties, every subject of civil law must respect certain ethical limits, in breach of which they enjoy no legal protection. More broadly, the principle of good faith aims to promote mutual loyalty, trust, and fairness in legal interaction.[248]

*121.* Thus, the principle of good faith prevents a situation in which civil-law subjects exercise their rights or perform their duties unjustifiably or for unreasonable purposes, acting by the text of a law or legal transaction, but contrary to its true purpose.[249] The exercise of a subjective right may be impermissible if the entitled person has no protected interests at all that would justify the exercise of the right, or the interests of the other party are considered to be more important.[250] Considering this in the context of tort law, it must be concluded that a person's exercise of subjective rights or performance of duties that causes damage to another person must be assessed in the light of the principle of good faith. A possible tortfeasor's unjustified exercise of their subjective rights or performance of duties may not enjoy legal protection (i.e., the possible tortfeasor may be held liable for damage caused while exercising their legal rights or performing duties) if it turns out that the tort victim's conflicting interests are more important in accordance with the purpose of the law and the circumstances of the case.[251]

## §4. Injury to Reputation and Privacy

*122.* Protection of a person's honour and dignity is normatively established in several legal acts. The right to protection of honour and dignity is envisaged as a fundamental right in Article 95 of the *Satversme*, which, among other things, presupposes that: 'The state shall protect human honour and dignity.' The general legal framework in civil law for the protection of this right can be found in Article 2352.[1] of the Civil Law, which protects each person's honour and dignity from injurious information if the disseminator of the information does not prove that such information is true. Since most cases regarding an injury to a person's honour and dignity are based on actions that have occurred through the mass media, the legislator

247. Balodis, K. (2007), *supra* n. 69, 141.lpp.; *see also* Balodis K. Labas ticības princips mūsdienu Latvijas civiltiesībās [*The Principle of Good Faith in Modern Latvian Civil Law*]. Jurista Vārds, 2002, Nr.24.
248. Balodis, K. (2002), *supra* n. 247.
249. Krons, M. Civīllikuma pirmais pants [*Article 1 of the Civil Law*]. Tieslietu Ministrijas Vēstnesis, 1937, Nr.2., 271.lpp; Balodis, K. (2007), *supra* n. 69, 141.lpp.
250. Balodis, K. (2002), *supra* n. 247.
251. Balodis, K. (2007), *supra* n. 69, 141.lpp.

has also imposed special obligations to protect a person's honour and dignity in the mass media.[252] For example, Article 7(5) of the Law on the Press and Other Mass Media states:

> Information that injures the honour and dignity of natural persons and juristic persons or defames them may not be published.

*123.* Latvian legislation, as indicated in these articles, normatively distinguishes honour and dignity as two separate objects of protection. Legal doctrine, as well as court practice, have followed the same approach, as is testified to by the following opinion:

> Honour and dignity are categories of ethics and morality, and each individual's understanding of them may differ. Honour is the social assessment of an individual that has developed as a result of the person's conduct, but dignity is the reflection of a person's public assessment in his own consciousness, i.e., the person's self-assessment.[253]

*124.* Settled court practice[254] of the Supreme Court demonstrates that Article 2352.[1] of the Civil Law is interpreted as not only protecting the honour and dignity of a natural person but also the reputation of legal persons, such as commercial companies, state capital companies, associations, and political parties.[255] This is also confirmed by an interpretation of the Law on the Press and Other Mass Media. The Supreme Court has acknowledged that, although only natural persons have dignity, from the textual scope of Article 7(5)[256] of the Law on the Press and Other Mass Media, it can be concluded that the legislator has extended the term 'honour' to the reputation of legal persons.[257]

*125.* The basis for applying for civil protection under Article 2352.[1] of the Civil Law arises if false, insulting information has been disseminated about a person. The court usually examines the merits of a claim brought under Article 2352.[1] of the

---

252. Torgāns, K., Kārkliņš, J., Bitāns, A. (2017), *supra* n. 70, 337.lpp.
253. Bitāns, A. Komentārs Civillikuma 2352.[1] pantam [*Commentary to Article 2352.[1] of the Civil Law*]. Grām.: Latvijas Republikas Civillikuma komentāri: Ceturtā daļa. Saistību tiesības [*Commentary on the Civil Law of the Republic of Latvia. Part Four. Law of Obligations*]. (2000), 635.lpp.
254. Some Latvian legal scholars use the recently introduced term 'judicature' (Latvian: *judikatūra*) as a synonym for characterization of settled court practice.
255. Augstākās tiesas prakses apkopojums 'Goda un cieņas civiltiesiskā aizsardzība (2000–2021.maijs)' [*Summary of the Supreme Court practice 'Civil protection of honour and dignity (May 2000–2021)*], 28.lpp. Available: https://at.gov.lv/files/uploads/files/6_Judikatura/Tiesu_prakses_apkopojumi/2021/goda_un_cienas_aizsardziba-2021(1).docx [accessed 30. Aug. 2021.].
256. As well as Art. 21(1), Art. 21(5), and Art. 28 Law on the Press and Other Mass Media. Official translation into English available on the official web-page of the State Language Centre at https://vvc.gov.lv/image/catalog/dokumenti/On%20the%20Press%20and%20Other%20Mass%20Media.docx [accessed on 17 Jan. 2022].
257. Judgment of the Supreme Court of 30 Apr. 2020 in Case No. SKC-77/2020 (C30450117), point 9.

Civil Law in accordance with a specific four-step procedure,[258] although in some situations, exceptions are and should be made.[259]

*126.* To determine the legal composition of this norm, the court must first establish that certain information has been disseminated in public and not in private to the aggrieved person. Tortious liability generally arises only when injurious information has been disseminated to a wider or not so wide circle of persons, but not only to the tort victim in person.[260]

*127.* Second, the court must assess whether the claim relates to (publicly available) information or opinion. As established in the settled court practice of the Supreme Court, liability for expressing an opinion does not fall within the scope of Article 2352.[1] of the Civil Law.[261] The need to distinguish information that injures honour and dignity from an unpleasant and offensive opinion stems from the obligation of the state to protect different fundamental rights – on the one hand, the right to protection of honour and dignity[262] and the right to privacy,[263] and, on the other hand, the right to freedom of expression[264] and the right to freedom of creative activity.[265]

*128.* Third, the court must assess whether the information disseminated is offensive to the claimant's honour and dignity. Honour and dignity are considered injured if it is established that, as a result of dissemination of false information, the public evaluation of a person and the reflection of the evaluation in the tort victim's own consciousness has decreased.[266] This aspect is assessed by taking into account the status of the person about whom the information has been disseminated. For example, the Supreme Court has acknowledged that the margin of tolerance for ordinary citizens is lower than for politicians, public officials, judges, board members of state capital companies, and the like.[267]

*129.* Finally to be ascertained is whether the disseminator of information cannot prove that the information is true. The claimant has to prove that the dissemination

258. Augstākās tiesas prakses apkopojums 'Goda un cieņas civiltiesiskā aizsardzība (2000–2021.maijs)' [*Summary of the Supreme Court practice 'Civil protection of honour and dignity (May 2000–2021)*], *supra* n. 255, 4.lpp.
259. Torgāns, K., Kārkliņš, J., Bitāns, A. (2017), *supra* n. 70, 339–350.lpp.
260. Augstākās tiesas prakses apkopojums 'Goda un cieņas civiltiesiskā aizsardzība (2000–2021.maijs)' [*Summary of the Supreme Court practice 'Civil protection of honour and dignity (May 2000–2021)*], *supra* n. 255, 4–5.lpp.
261. Judgment of the Supreme Court of 21 Feb. 2017 in Case No. SKC-26/2017 (C30706512), point 7.
262. Article 95 *Satversme*, *supra* n. 43.
263. Article 96 *Satversme*, *supra* n. 43.
264. Article 100 *Satversme*, *supra* n. 43.
265. Article 113 *Satversme*, *supra* n. 43; Augstākās tiesas prakses apkopojums 'Goda un cieņas civiltiesiskā aizsardzība (2000–2021.maijs)' [*Summary of the Supreme Court practice 'Civil protection of honuor and dignity (May 2000–2021)*], *supra* n. 255, 8.lpp.
266. Augstākās tiesas prakses apkopojums 'Goda un cieņas civiltiesiskā aizsardzība (2000–2021.maijs)' [*Summary of the Supreme Court Senate practice 'Civil protection of honour and dignity (May 2000–2021)*], *supra* n. 255, 14.lpp.
267. *Ibid.*, 19.lpp.

of information has injured their honour and dignity. The defendant, however, if disputing the claim, has the burden of proof as to the truthfulness of the information, i.e., the defendant has to prove that the disseminated information is true.[268] The truthfulness of the disseminated information must be considered in light of the fact that information can be proved to be false after it has been disseminated. The Supreme Court, referring to the court practice of the European Court of Human Rights, has recognized that a journalist cannot be held liable for the dissemination of information of public interest which was subsequently proved to be false if, at the time of dissemination or publication, the journalist acted in good faith and could have had full confidence that the information was true.[269] Thus, in specific situations, a person may be released from liability for the dissemination of false information that has injured a person's honour and dignity.

*130.* In cases of injury to a person's honour and dignity, general civil remedies are available. For example, Article 2352.[1] of the Civil Law gives a tort victim the right to compensation for pecuniary and non-pecuniary damage. This legal norm also presupposes specific civil remedies, such as retraction of false information. If a tort has been committed through the mass media, then, in addition to the general remedies provided for in the Civil Law, remedies provided for in special legal acts are applicable, such as an apology.[270]

*131.* The right to privacy, similarly to a person's right to protection of honour and dignity, is recognized as a fundamental right. Article 96 of the *Satversme* states that: 'Everyone has the right to inviolability of his private life, home, and correspondence.' Besides this legal norm of constitutional rank, protection of privacy is regulated in a large number of other legal acts, although the term 'privacy' is not found in them. These legal acts include the Civil Law, the Criminal Law, the Postal Law, the Archives Law, the Personal Data Processing Law, among others.[271]

*132.* As noted in legal doctrine, in addition to civil liability for invasion of privacy, either criminal or administrative liability may arise. Legal doctrine differentiates several forms of privacy, such as (1) housing privacy, (2) privacy of personal life, (3) privacy of secrets, (4) privacy of correspondence, (5) reputational privacy, and (6) children's privacy.[272] The type of liability, the preconditions for establishing liability, and remedies for damage to a person's privacy are differentiated depending on which form of privacy is involved.

*133.* As in other countries, the most common civil remedy in Latvia for injury to a person's privacy is compensation for pecuniary and non-pecuniary damage.

268. *Ibid.*, 21–22.lpp.
269. *Ibid.*, 22.lpp.
270. Art. 21(1) Law on the Press and Other Mass Media, *supra* n. 256; Torgāns, K., Kārkliņš, J., Bitāns, A. (2017), *supra* n. 70, 349.lpp.
271. Torgāns, K., Kārkliņš, J., Bitāns, A. (2017), *supra* n. 70, 351.lpp.
272. Ibid., 369–372.lpp.

However, in addition, the following could also be used as remedies in case of invasion of privacy: restoration of the victim's previous situation (restitution); recognition of invasion of privacy; termination of the infringement; imposition of an obligation to further refrain from performing this type of activity or to take certain action in order not to infringe privacy; and prevention of unjust enrichment.[273]

## §5. Interference by a Third Person with Contractual Relations

*134*. Under the Latvian legal framework, contractual relations, like tort relations, are formed as relative legal relations,[274] and thus generally concern only the parties to a particular legal transaction. However, third persons must, in principle, respect contractual legal relations so that unlawful interference with contractual relations can give rise to a third person's civil liability under the general grounds presupposed in the Civil Law. Third persons can be held liable, for example, for unlawfully impeding the fulfilment of contractual obligations. Nevertheless, in some circumstances, interference may be permissible. As an example, interference by a third person with contractual relations may be permissible in situations regarding absolutely invalid legal transactions, for example, fictitious transactions.[275] A third person whose civil rights or legally protected interests have been infringed by a fictitious transaction has the right to bring a court action to establish the absolute invalidity of the particular legal transaction.[276]

273. *Ibid.*, 372.lpp.
274. Torgāns, K. (2018), *supra* n. 11, 17.lpp.
275. Article 1438 CL.
276. Balodis, K. (2007), *supra* n. 69, 187–188.lpp.; Judgment of the Supreme Court of Latvia of 28 Sep. 2018 in Case No. SKC-207/2018 (C27207010), point 13.2.

# Part II. Liability for Acts of Others

## Chapter 1. Vicarious Liability

### §1. EMPLOYEE/EMPLOYER

*135.* As a general principle, everyone has an obligation to compensate damage they cause by their acts or omissions.[277] However, as recognized in legal doctrine[278] and court practice, 'in some cases, responsibilities may be shared between the tortfeasor and the people supervising him in a certain way'.[279] The Supreme Court, in reference to the court practice of the interwar period Senate (equivalent to the Supreme Court nowadays), has noted that:

> the duty to carefully select servants and employees, as well as their supervision, lies with all masters, since anyone who uses other person's services for their own needs is also obliged to take risks in a certain way for the unauthorised activities permitted by those persons in the performance of their duties. The question of what conditions should be met for the selection of servants or employees and what steps should be taken to monitor them, must be decided by court, considering the nature of the task, its dangers and the precautionary requirements normally imposed. In addition, the obligation of choice and supervision and, consequently, the responsibility of the owner are to the extent that the obligation imposed on servants or employees is likely to cause damage to third parties. The supervisor shall be liable for damage caused by his servant to third parties only if he has not taken the necessary care in selecting the servants or if he was obliged or able, through appropriate supervision, to influence the occurrence of the damage.[280]

*136.* Article 1782 of the Civil Law imposes an obligation to pay due attention to selection of servants and other employees and to ascertain their ability and usefulness to perform the duties imposed on them. A person who fails to perform this duty

277. Article 1779 CL.
278. Torgāns, K. Komentārs Civillikuma 1782.pantam [*Commentary of Article 1782 of the Civil Law*]. Grām.: Latvijas Republikas Civillikuma komentāri: Ceturtā daļa. Saistību tiesības [*Commentary to the Civil Law of the Republic of Latvia: Part four. Law of Obligations*]. (2000), 275.lpp.
279. Judgment of the Supreme Court of 29 Dec. 2016 in Case No. SKC-368/2016 (C29459809), point 11.
280. *Ibid.*, point 12.

properly will be blamed for their choice of employee.[281] Legal doctrine states that this norm was not initially intended for the liability of legal persons for their employees, but nowadays, it can also be applied to determine the liability of an employer, including a legal person, for damage caused by an employee because a legal person must also carefully select its employees and, if they prove incapable or unqualified in terms of the obligations imposed, then the legal person will be liable for damage. This regulation is based on the consideration that persons who employ others in order to achieve an economic objective must also be responsible for the risks arising from the employment of those persons.[282]

*137.* However, the same fault that can be found in an employee, which can be both negligence and wrongful intent, cannot be considered as an employer's responsibility but it should be considered as a specific form of fault – fault in choice. As noted in Part I of this monograph *supra*, an employer's liability in Latvia is not based on strict liability, as the employer had the right to prove that it had tested the employee's abilities and usefulness.[283] In other words, if the employer is able to prove that there is no ordinary negligence on its part (in its choice of employee) or that its conduct complies with the 'prudent and careful person' clause, then no liability arises. Article 831(1) of the German Civil Code (BGB)[284] provides for a regulation similar to Article 1782 of the Civil Law, i.e., the employer is released from liability if it proves that there is no ordinary negligence in its selection of employees.[285]

*138.* The fact that an employee has committed a faulty action does not automatically mean that responsibility for infringing rights can be applied to the employer. It is necessary to establish that the employer has committed at least ordinary negligence in selecting the employee. In addition, it must be noted that the employee has committed a faulty action in the performance of their duties.[286] The employer will not be liable in a civil action if an employee strikes a pedestrian with his car during training leave, even though the employee is paid a salary for that time.

*139.* Note that Article 1782 of the Civil Law is applicable only in cases when an employee infringes the rights of third persons. If an employee fails to perform a client's contract on behalf of the employer, the employer is liable for breach of contract even if it cannot be blamed for the selection of the employee. In court practice, a false conclusion is often found, according to which Article 1782 of the Civil Law applies in cases where work has been performed on the basis of a contract of employment. However, in the court practice of the Supreme Court, this assumption has been found to be false. Work for the benefit of another person may be carried

281. Torgāns, K., Kārkliņš, J. (2015), *supra* n. 117.
282. Kubilis, J. (2016), *supra* n. 78, 235.lpp.
283. Zimmermann, R. *The Law of Obligations: Roman Foundations of the Civilian Tradition*. Oxford, New York: Oxford University Press, 1996, p.377.
284. English translation of the BGB available at www.gesetze-im-internet.de/englisch_bgb/index.html [accessed on 28 Jun. 2021].
285. Torgāns, K., Kārkliņš, J. (2015), *supra* n. 117.
286. Kubilis, J. (2016), *supra* n. 78, 235.lpp.

out not only on the basis of a contract of employment but also on the basis of a contract for work performance. The provisions of a contract for work performance in the Civil Law can be found in the chapter titled 'Claims from Work Relations'. Under Article 2212(2) of the Civil Law, the provisions regarding employment contracts are applicable to contracts for work performance, insofar as those provisions are not in conflict with the following articles.[287] In addition, legal doctrine commentating on Article 1782 of the Civil Law states that participants in civil proceedings may, for the performance of their duties and obligations, attract assistants on the basis of a contract of employment, a contract for work performance or subcontracting.[288]

*140.* Article 1782 of the Civil Law applies only in cases where damage has been caused to third parties.[289] In addition, there is a presumption of fault under Article 1782 of the Civil Law. In this regard, the interwar period Senate indicated that Article 1782 of the Civil Law establishes an independent basis for the liability of a supervisor. Thus, a supervisor is liable for damage caused by their servant unless they can prove that violation of the rights of the victim is not the supervisor's fault.[290] According to the court practice of the interwar period Senate, an employer that compensates the victim for damages on the basis of Article 1782 of the Civil Law does not lose its right to reclaim those damages from the direct perpetrator.[291]

*141.* The regulatory framework of the Labour Law, as a special law in contrast to the Civil Law, allows an employer to deduct damages caused to it due to the illegal conduct of an employee.[292] This special legal norm, unlike Article 1782 of the Civil Law, is applicable only in cases where damages have been caused directly to

---

287. Judgment of the Supreme Court of 29 Dec. 2016 in Case No. SKC-368/2016 (C29459809), point 15.
288. Torgāns, K. (2018), *supra* n. 11, 202.lpp.
289. *Senāta 1933.gada 25.novembra spriedums Nr. 117.* X Izvilkumi no Latvijas Senāta Civilā kasācijas departamenta spriedumiem. Sastādījuši: senators Konradi F. Un Rīgas apgabaltiesas loceklis Valters A. [*Judgment of the Senate No. 117 of 25 Nov. 1933. X Extracts from the judgments of the Civil Cassation Department of the Latvian Senate. Compiled by: Senator Konradi F. and member of the Riga Regional Court Valters A.*]. Rīga: Autoru izdevums, 1933, 224., 225.lpp.
290. *Senāta Apvienotās Sapulces 1937.gada 29.novembra spriedums Nr. 33.* XIV Izvilkumi no Latvijas Senāta Civilā kasācijas departamenta spriedumiem. Sastādījuši: senators Konradi F. un Rīgas apgabaltiesas loceklis Valters A. [*Judgment No. 33 of the Joint Assembly of the Senate of 29 Nov. 1937. XIV Extracts from Judgments of the Civil Cassation Department of the Latvian Senate. Compiled by: Senator Konradi F. and member of the Riga Regional Court Valters A.*]. Rīga: Tieslietu ministrijas izdevums, 1938, 79.lpp.
291. *Senāta 1932.gada 26.oktobra spriedums Nr. 841.* IX Izvilkumi no Latvijas Senāta Civilā kasācijas departamenta spriedumiem. Sastādījuši: senators Konradi F. un Rīgas apgabaltiesas loceklis Valters A. [*Judgment of the Senate No. 841 of 26 Oct. 1932. IX Extracts from the judgments of the Civil Cassation Department of the Latvian Senate. Compiled by: Senator Konradi F. and member of the Riga Regional Court Valters A.*]. Rīga: Autoru izdevums, 1932, 309.lpp.
292. Article 79 of the Labour Law states: 'An employer has the right to deduct from the remuneration to be disbursed to an employee compensation for losses caused thereto due to an illegal, culpable action by the employee. The making of such deduction requires written consent from the employee.' Official translation into English available on the official web-page of the State Language Centre at https://vvc.gov.lv/image/catalog/dokumenti/Labour%20Law.docx [accessed on 17 Jan. 2022].

the employer due to illegal action by an employee. In order for the employer to be entitled to deduct damages from the employee's salary, the following obligations must be accepted as preconditions: (1) the existence of damage(s); (2) the cause of the damage(s) is the employee's illegal action; (3) the employee has agreed in writing to make the deductions from salary. If any of these preconditions do not exist, the employer may not make deductions from pay. Even if an employee's illegal action is detected, the written consent of the employee to make such a deduction is also required.[293] However, if an employee contests the basis or the amount of a claim for compensation of damage caused to the employer, the employer may bring an action in court within two years from the day the damage was caused.[294]

*142.* A similar framework for determining liability can be found in Article 1638 of the Civil Law. This provision states that a subordinate who commits a tort pursuant to the orders of his supervisor will not be held liable if the act is not itself criminal. It does not matter whether the employee is aware of the illegality of the order. No person can plead ignorance of a criminal offence under the Criminal Law. It is possible that the supervisor may have given the order with wrongful intent and negligently, ignoring the possible consequences.[295] If, however, a criminal offence has been committed in accordance with the given task, then the liability of the employee and the employer is determined under Article 1675 of the Civil Law.[296] The truth of the above is also confirmed by Article 1639 of the Civil Law, which stipulates that a person who allows a tort to take place will be liable for it in circumstances where, as the employer, has the opportunity, and therefore the duty, to prevent such a tort.

## §2. Independent Contractors

*143.* An independent contractor is usually considered as a natural person or entity contracted to perform work for – or provide services to – another entity as a non-employee. Legal relations between the independent contractor and another entity are usually established by a contract for work performance, the definition of which is provided in Article 2212 of the Civil Law.[297]

293. Komentārs Darba likuma 79.pantam [*Commentary to Article 79 of the Labour Law*]. Grām.: Latvijas Brīvo arodbiedrību savienība, Zvērinātu advokātu birojs 'BDO Law'. Darba likums ar komentāriem [*Latvian Free Trade Union Confederation, Sword Advocate Office 'BDO Law'. Labour Law with commentary*]. Izdevējs: Latvijas Brīvo arodbiedrību savienība, 2020, 214.lpp.
294. Article 79(2) Labour Law, *supra* n. 292.
295. Torgāns, K., Kārkliņš, J., Bitāns, A. (2017), *supra* n. 70, 313.lpp.
296. Article 1675 Civil Law states: 'If a criminal offence has been committed jointly by more than one person, they shall be solidarily (jointly and severally [authors' comment]) liable for losses caused thereby.'
297. Article 2212 Civil Law states: 'Pursuant to a contract for work-performance, one party undertakes, using the party's tools and equipment and for a certain remuneration, to perform for another party an order, the production of some product or the conducting to its completion of some activity.' For a general discussion of work performance in Latvian civil law, *see* Torgāns, K., Kārkliņš, J., Mantrov, V., Rasnačs, L. (2020), *supra* n. 4, p.216 et seq.

*144.* First of all, it should be noted that *culpa in eligendo* in the context of independent contractors can be twofold. Namely, *culpa in eligendo* in that context can take the form of both the fault of the commissioning party in the choice of independent contractor and the fault of the independent contractor in their choice of subcontractor. As previously noted, the liability of an independent contractor or the commissioning party for damage caused to third parties is regulated by Article 1782 of the Civil Law. This imposes an obligation to pay due attention to the selection of servants and other employees and to ascertain their ability and usefulness to perform the duties imposed on them.

*145.* The liability of the independent contractor is regulated in Article 2217(3) of the Civil Law, which states:

> The contractor shall also compensate for losses where the contractor is at fault as a result of his own incompetence or in the situation where he or she employs incompetent or careless help or help that acts in bad faith.

*146.* An independent contractor must observe the so-called utmost diligence (*omnis diligentia*) and is not responsible only for unavoidable cases (*cas fortuit*). In this respect, relations between an independent contractor and their servant (subcontractor), on the one hand, and between the independent contractor and the commissioning party, on the other hand, should not be subject to the general Article 1782 of the Civil Law, but to the special Article 2217 of the same law. This also makes an independent contractor liable for the recklessness of their selected servants, i.e., for their negligence. Article 2217 of the Civil Law, unlike Article 1782, does not oblige the victim to prove the fault of an independent contractor in *culpa in eligendo*. Article 2217 of the Civil Law establishes the liability of an independent contractor when the negligence of the servant (subcontractor) as such has been proved.[298]

*147.* In any case, the contractor bears the risk of non-performance. The nature of the contract may give rise to the right to have assistants. However, it must be emphasized that the risk and all responsibility is borne by the contractor even if the work has been performed by a third party engaged by the contractor.[299] The truth of this is also confirmed by the findings of court practice.[300]

---

298. *Senāta 1923.gada 26.aprīļa spriedums Nr. 141.* II Izvilkumi no Latvijas Senāta Civilā kasācijas departamenta spriedumiem. Sastādījuši: senators Konradi F. Un Rīgas apgabaltiesas loceklis Valters A [*Senate Judgment No. 141 of 26 Apr. 1923. II Extracts from Judgments of the Civil Cassation Department of the Latvian Senate. Compiled by: Senator Konradi F. and member of the Riga Regional Court Valters A.*]. Rīga: Autoru izdevums, 1926, 56.lpp.

299. Torgāns, K. Komentārs Civillikuma 2217.pantam [*Commentary to Article 2217 of the Civil Law*]. Grām.: Latvijas Republikas Civillikuma komentāri: Ceturtā daļa. Saistību tiesības [*Commentary to the Civil Law of the Republic of Latvia: Part four. Law of Obligations*]. (2000), 528.lpp.

300. Judgment of the Riga Regional Court of 17 Nov. 2020 in Case No. C29461816, point 14.3.2.

*148.* It follows from a contractor's undertaking to perform the contract that they consider themselves expert in the field of work in question. It follows that the contractor assumes the risks of achieving or failing to achieve the necessary end result. A contract for work performance is characterized by the independence of the contractor, the type of performance of the activity, methods, sequences, and so on, selection, assessment of material quality and application. However, certain instructions for execution of the order may be included in the contract, while the customer (commissioning party) may give instructions in the course of the work without violating the independence of the contractor. The contractor, as an expert, must be able to evaluate the customer's instructions, taking into account that it is the contractor's responsibility to give a quality end result.[301]

## §3. Liability of Legal Entities for Acts of Their Institutions

*149.* Legal capacity of legal entities is exercised by the institutions of a legal person. Legal persons have the capacity to act and are liable in tort. Legal persons are only able to acquire rights and assume obligations if natural persons are acting on their behalf. Under Article 1410(2) of the Civil Law, legal transactions are concluded on behalf of legal persons through their legal representatives. Without the participation of natural persons as legal representatives, legal persons cannot perform any legally significant activities. In general, a legal representative can be both a natural person and a legal person. However, legal persons themselves can be represented and managed only by natural persons in the form of bodies of the legal person. Depending on the specifics of the type and structure of a legal entity, they are formed by one natural person or a group of several natural persons (e.g., board member, council). The will of the institutions of a legal person is formed on the basis of collective or individual decisions under the procedures prescribed by law and/or the (company) statutes. Actions by the institutions of a legal person are the actions of the legal person itself, and they may only act within the scope of their competence specified by law and the (company) statutes.[302] For example, under Article 209 of the KCL, the institutions of a limited liability company are the meeting of shareholders and the board, as well as the council (if formed). Article 221 of the KCL, revealing the legal definition of the concept of the board, states that the board is the executive institution of a legal person which directs and represents the legal person in relations with other legal entities or natural persons.[303]

*150.* As indicated in the legal literature, management of a legal person covers the obligation of a board member to ensure the activities of the legal person, including taking organizational measures to ensure the development of commercial activities, ensuring the functioning of the company, in accordance with the requirements of the law, giving orders to employees, taking decisions, keeping accounting

301. Torgāns, K. (2018), *supra* n. 11, 350.lpp.
302. Balodis, K. (2007), *supra* n. 69, 93.lpp.
303. Bērziņš, J. Komercsabiedrības amatpersonu civiltiesiskās atbildības aspekti [*Aspects of Civil Liability of Officials of a Commercial Company*]. Jurista Vārds, 2009, Nr.19.

records, and taking other necessary measures to ensure the commercial activities of the company. However, the representation of the legal person refers to its representation in 'outside' relations in terms of relations with third parties, such as conclusion of a transaction and submission of documents.[304]

*151.* A tort by a legal person may be expressed in such a way that the legal person is always liable with its property for damage caused to other persons by the institutions of the legal person. Thus, as in the case of legal transactions, the conduct of the bodies of a legal person is to be regarded as that of the legal person itself. Consequently, the fault of the institutions of a legal person is to be regarded as that of the legal person itself. In that light, it should be noted that Article 1782 of the Civil Law is not quite applicable in determining the tortious liability of a legal person for the acts of its institutions. The essence of a legal person is to separate the liability of its members from the liability of the legal person itself. This principle also works vice-versa – a participant (shareholder) is not liable for a legal person's obligations (contractual or non-contractual), but the legal person is also not liable for the participant's obligations.[305] In view of the fact that the activities of institutions of a legal person are considered to be the activities of legal persons themselves, their fault in wrongful activity will be considered to be the fault of the legal person itself. Thus, in the case of a wrongful act, both a legal person and its institutions share the same form of fault. However, within the meaning of Article 1782 of the Civil Law, a servant and their supervisor share different forms of fault – the supervisor is at fault for the negligence in choice of a servant, while a servant is at fault for the wrongful act itself.

*152.* The Civil Law does not contain a literal indication that the tort liability of the institutions of legal person is automatically attributable to the legal person itself. A legal person is a subject of civil law, comparable in terms of rights and obligations to natural persons. It is, therefore, logical that legal persons should also be liable for non-contractual infringements (i.e., torts). Since a legal person has no legal capacity without the participation of natural persons, it is therefore responsible for the unlawful conduct of its executive organs which consist of those natural persons.[306]

*153.* In certain cases regulated by the KCL, the institutions of a legal person are themselves responsible for damage caused to the legal person. However, the understanding of whether this liability of board members is contractual or tortious varies in different legal systems. For example, in Italy, Poland, Norway, and Turkey, the institute of board member liability are recognized as a form of contractual liability,

---

304. Lielkalne, B. Valdes locekļu nodarbinātības problemātiskie aspekti [*Problematic Aspects of Employment of Board Members*]. Jurista Vārds, 2012, Nr.9.

305. Strupišs, A. Komentārs Komerclikuma 137.pantam [*Commentary to Article 137 of the Commercial Law*]. Grām.: Strupišs A. Komerclikuma komentāri III. B daļa. Komersanti. XI sadaļa. Kapitālsabiedrības (134–184.panti) [*Commentary to the Commercial Law III. Part B. Merchants. Section XI. Capital companies (Articles 134–184)*]. Rīga: SIA 'A. Strupiša juridiskais birojs', 2003, 30–31.lpp.

306. Balodis, K. (2007), *supra* n. 69, 95.lpp.

while in Israel, it is recognized as a form of tortious liability.[307] However, in Latvia (similarly to what is recognized in German and Austrian legal doctrine), there would be more reason to speak of the fact that the concept of liability of a board member is a specific institute of liability provided by law.[308] Indirectly, such a finding is expressed in a judgment of the Supreme Court,[309] recognizing that the obligation of a board member to compensate the company for damages is set by law and is established in each specific case by a court judgment.[310]

307. Novicāne, E. (2021), *supra* n. 160., 29–32.lpp.
308. Article 1402 CL.
309. Judgment of the Supreme Court of 21 Dec. 2015 in Case No. SKC-251/2015 (C03011111), point 8.
310. Novicāne, E. (2021), *supra* n. 160.

## Chapter 2. Liability of Parents, Teachers, and Instructors

*154.* It should first of all be noted that the general principle of liability for actions of others is defined by the Civil Law itself. Article 1639 of the Civil Law states that:

> A person who allows a delict ['delict'= 'tort': authors' note] to take place shall be liable for it in circumstances where, due to his personal relationship with the transgressor, as one of the parents or as the supervisor, he has the opportunity, and therefore the duty, to prevent such a tort.

*155.* As is clear from the quoted provision, in those cases where a special personal relationship can be established between a person who has committed a tort and the person whose obligation it was to supervise them, civil liability may arise for the supervising person on the grounds of insufficient supervision. However, that liability under Article 1639 of the Civil Law will not in any way affect the liability of the person who committed the tort. Essentially the civil liability of the two persons arises on different grounds and is therefore not to be considered together but separately from each other – these persons are not jointly civilly liable. Consequently, the victim of a tort can either bring several claims against both persons simultaneously or choose only one person and one ground under which to attempt to obtain compensation. In this regard, we note that a person cannot receive full satisfaction from both persons. In this case, there would be evidence of unjust enrichment.[311]

*156.* To examine the liability of parents, teachers, instructors, and other persons who are generally liable for the actions of those who are incapable of fully comprehending the consequences of their actions, we first need to define the *circle of persons* whose activities are *under supervision of others* within the meaning of the Civil Law. This circle of persons is mainly regulated by Article 1780 of the Civil Law.[312] This provision states the list of those to be supervised includes children not over 7 years of age and persons with disorders of a mental nature, who are not able to understand their actions. According to this provision, negligence by supervisors forms an independent basis for the duty to compensate for damage caused. In these

311. For a general discussion of unjust enrichment in Latvia, *see* Torgāns, K., Kārkliņš, J., Mantrov, V., Rasnačs, L. (2020), *supra* n. 4, p.267 et seq.

312. Article 1780 CL states: 'Losses that have been caused by children who are not more than seven years of age, by a person with disorders of a mental nature, who was not able to understand the meaning of his action or was not able to control his action, or by a person having capacity to act but when the person is in a state of unconsciousness or being unable to understand the meaning of his action or being unable to control his action, shall be compensated from the property of these persons to the extent that they are not deprived of means needed for their maintenance. If losses have occurred because of the negligence of a person whose duty it is to supervise the aforementioned persons, such person shall be primarily liable regarding the losses to the extent of his own property.'

circumstances, when the negligence of parents, guardians and the like can be found, they are not responsible for the wrongful actions of those they are supervising, but for their own negligent actions.[313]

*157.* Accordingly, it is essential to differentiate the age of a minor that has committed a tort under Article 1780 of the Civil Law. Persons who have not reached the age of seven cannot be held accountable for their doings, as they do not have tortious liability, which is not to say that property owned by them generally cannot be used to pay for damage caused. Under Article 1780 of the Civil Law, damage caused by persons under the age of 7 is to be compensated mainly from their property to the extent that they are not deprived of the means needed for their maintenance.

*158.* When liability of schools or parents is under consideration, it should be noted that in these cases *fault* of these subjects is *presumed*. At the same time, it would be incorrect to conclude that there is a strict liability model in these cases. Article 1639 of the Civil Law states that a person may be released from liability if they prove that there is no lack of diligence on their part, in other words, absence of negligence may be a ground to avoid liability. Thus fault is one of the preconditions that has to be established for the application of parental responsibility. This means that although parental fault is presumed, this presumption can be rebutted.[314]

*159.* If it is concluded that damage has occurred because of the negligence of a person whose duty it is to supervise, the victim will be compensated first by the property of the supervisor(s), but if that is not enough, then compensation may be covered from the property of the person because of whom the damage occurred.[315] In that light, it is worth examining on whom the burden of proof lies in these circumstances. In situations like those analysed before, it is generally accepted that the burden of proof for establishing the absence of negligence lies upon parents. This is largely due to the fact that it is easier for parents, if they have taken all reasonable measures, to prove the existence of their own reasonable care than for a person who has been the victim of a tort. The victim of a tort may also be unaware of the personal circumstances of the family in question, which may be relevant in establishing a lack of diligence.[316] In any case, the persons mentioned in Article 1780 of the Civil Law (children under the age of seven and persons with disorders of a mental nature) cannot be liable in tort, as they lack capacity for tortious liability, but their property can still be used for compensation under the circumstances mentioned in this provision.

*160.* The legal situation is different in the case of persons over the age of 7 but who still have not reached majority. First, we should note that these persons can be liable for their own actions, and they can be defendants in court (although their

---

313. Буковскій, В. (1914), *supra* n. 150, c.1403.
314. Torgāns, K., Kārkliņš, J., Bitāns, A. (2017), *supra* n. 70, 312.lpp.
315. Bitāns, A. Civiltiesiskā atbildība un tās veidi [*Civil Liability and Its Types*]. Rīga: Izdevniecība AGB, 1997, 84.lpp.
316. Буковскій, В. (1914), *supra* n. 150, c.1402.

rights will be defended by their representatives).[317] In addition, there is no explicit exception that would allow for compensation of damage caused to be compensated first by their supervisors. In other words, persons over the age of 7 are independently liable and must cover damage caused by their own property.

*161.* Article 1639 of the Civil Law could be also applied regarding teachers and instructors as it could be said that their duty to supervise is established by law. For example, Article 68 of the Law on the Protection of the Children's Rights states that it is the duty of educational and other institutions to ensure children's rights and maintain order in these institutions. If supervision is insufficient and pupils cause damage to others, there would be no reason not to apply Article 1639 of the Civil Law to these circumstances as relationships between pupils and school administration (i.e., teachers) could be seen as personal in the meaning of Article 1639.

*162.* In regard to Article 1639 of the Civil Law, we should also note that the duty to prevent tort is not the same as the duty of supervisors to watch over others as stated in Article 1780 of the Civil Law. It would be incorrect to conclude that under Article 1639 of the Civil Law, parents or supervisors must be held liable for any tort committed by those under their supervision.[318] The standard of supervision contained in that article is lower. For example, it would not be reasonable to hold a parent liable if a child accidentally breaks a window while playing ball in a stadium. The situation would be different, however, if a generally rebellious child, who, with permission from their parents, went out on a Friday night and damaged the neighbours' windows. In these circumstances, because the child was generally rebellious, the parents should have predicted that such an outcome could occur. In these circumstances, negligence by the parents would be a basis of liability under Article 1639 of the Civil Law.

*163.* It would be also worth mentioning that the general principle 'those who do not understand their actions will not be liable for them' is also established in the Civil Law, whose Article 1637 states:

> Children under seven years of age, as well as persons with disorders of a mental nature or other health disorders, who are not able to understand the meaning of their actions or are not able to control their actions, shall not be held liable for them.

However, this rule does not apply in those cases when persons have self-induced a state of unconsciousness by alcohol or other means (Article 1637(2) of the Civil Law) and in no way does that same article affects the liability of supervisors as already described.[319]

---

317. Article 72(2) and (3) CPL.
318. Буковскій, B. (1914), *supra* n. 150, c.1301.
319. Torgāns, K. Komentārs Civillikuma 1637.pantam [*Commentary to Article 1637 of the Civil Law*]. Grām.: Latvijas Republikas Civillikuma komentāri: Ceturtā daļa. Saistību tiesības [*Commentary to the Civil Law of the Republic of Latvia: Part Four. Law of Obligations*]. (2000), 146.lpp.

## Chapter 3. Liability for Things and Animals

*164.* Liability arising from damage caused by things under Latvian law can be seen from the standpoint of two perspectives.

*165.* On the one hand, damage caused by things can occur because of incomplete fulfilment of a contract. For example, if a seller sells a defective axe and the head of the axe falls off, as a result of breaking a vase, it could be said that the seller is responsible not for a tort committed, but for incomplete fulfilment of a purchase contract. As these cases do not create liability based on tort, but rather liability arising from contract, they will not be further examined.

*166.* On the other hand, the Civil Law holds that a person can be held liable for damage caused by things put under their responsibility. Interestingly, Article 1038 of the Civil Law envisages that:

> An owner may possess property belonging to him, acquire the fruits thereof, use it at his discretion for the increase of his property and, generally, use it in any manner whatsoever, even if losses are caused thereby to other persons.

*167.* A verbatim reading of this provision could give the false impression that the owner can handle their property in any way they wish. This provision is largely based on the Ancient Roman understanding of property, along with all the selfish elements of that era regarding property. All the following articles of the Civil Law essentially make complete freedom of the owner illusory. Actions by the owner, as a result of which damage may be caused to another person, are primarily significantly limited by the general limits on use of property and, in particular, Article 1 of the Civil Law, which establishes that all rights have to be exercised in good faith in regard to others.[320] In that light, it should be said that Article 1038 of the Civil Law in no way limits the rights of a victim to claim compensation or even their right to demand cessation of conduct with one's property that is contrary to the principle of good faith.[321]

*168.* As for damage caused by things, it should also be noted that the Civil Law provides specific regulation in terms of damage caused by objects which are thrown, fallen, or poured. This kind of damage is a result of non-compliance with Article 1084 of the Civil Law, i.e., non-compliance with an obligation and responsibility to keep the property in such a condition as to prevent possible threats to third parties.[322] Article 2358 of the Civil Law states that:

---

320. Grūtups, A., Kalniņš, E. Komentārs Civillikuma 1038.pantam [*Commentary to Article 1038 of the Civil Law*]. Grām.: Grūtups, A. Kalniņš, E. Civillikuma komentāri. Trešā daļa. Lietu tiesības. Īpašums [*Commentary to the Civil Law. Third part. Property rights. Property*]. Rīga: Tiesu namu aģentūra, 2002, 181.lpp
321. Krons, M. (1937), *supra* n. 249.
322. Judgment of the Supreme Court of 21 Nov. 2016 in Case No. SKC-351/2016, point 6.1.

> If loss is caused by something being thrown or poured out into the street or another place where people walk or stay, or by inadequately fastened objects falling from a house onto the street, etc., a person suffering such loss may claim compensation for the loss from a person indicated in Article 2359.

*169.* This article further notes that compensation from damage under Article 2358 may not be claimed by the owner of a building, but *first by a person living in it or having*, for whatever reason, possession of the building or that part of the building from which something was poured or thrown. It seems worth noting that, under Article 2360(2) of the Civil Law, if the same building is occupied by several persons, they are held liable for damage as joint debtors, but any of them who pays more than their share may claim recovery of the overpaid amount from the others. Also, it is worth noting that claims arising from this kind of tort are proscribed after one year from the time the tort occurs (Article 2362 of the Civil Law).[323]

*170.* Damage caused by animals is also considered as one of the types of liability for damage caused by the properties of an object. Pets under the Civil Law may be an object of property, except for special cases specified by law.[324] Wild animals, however, can be acquired as property by way of appropriation. Only if the owner has left an animal or abandoned it may a pet become ownerless property.[325] However, some limitations on acquisition of animals can be found in the Animal Protection Law, which prohibits ownership of certain species.

*171.* Under Article 934 of the Civil Law, pets are not considered to be without an owner even when they escape or stray. Under Article 2363 of the Civil Law, the holder of pets or wild animals is responsible for damage caused by them if they do not prove that they have taken all necessary reasonable safety precautions in the circumstances or that the damage would have occurred despite all security measures.[326] It is worth mentioning that certain aspects of the duties of guardians, supervisors and owners of animals can be found in the Animal Protection Law. [327] Under Article 2366 of the Civil Law, an owner who has entrusted an animal to a guardian or supervisor will be liable for all damage, but the liability of the owner occurs only in the event of the guardian's insolvency. The *fault* of the person responsible in such a case is *presumed* on the assumption that the person responsible has not paid the increased or special attention required for that pet or wild animal, a presumption that can be rebutted only by proving that the responsible person has taken

323. Bitāns, A. (1997), *supra* n. 315, 127.lpp.
324. Grūtups, A., Kalniņš, E. Komentārs Civillikuma 929.pantam [*Commentary to Article 929 of the Civil Law*]. Grām.: Grūtups, A. Kalniņš, E. Civillikuma komentāri. Trešā daļa. Lietu tiesības. Īpašums [*Commentary to the Civil Law. The third part. Property rights. Property*]. Rīga: Tiesu namu aģentūra, 2002, 34.lpp.
325. Rozenfelds, J. Lietu tiesības. 4.labotais, papildinātais izdevums [*Property rights. 4th revised, supplemented edition*]. Autora redakcijā. Rīga: Zvaigzne ABC, 2011, 81.lpp.
326. Judgment of the Supreme Court of 31 Mar. 2014 in Case No. SKC-0061/14, point 7.1.
327. *See*, e.g., Art. 5 Animal Protection Law. Official translation into English available on the official web-page of the State Language Centre at https://vvc.gov.lv/image/catalog/dokumenti/Animal%20Protection%20Law.docx [accessed on 17 Jan. 2022].

all possible and necessary security measures.[328] In these cases, the victim (the claimant in court proceedings) has only to prove that the damage has indeed occurred and that there is both a factual and a legal relationship between the damage and the defendant. The presumption of fault is usually established by the legislator in those legal relations in which information about the violation and the related facts is more accessible to the infringer, so that rebuttal of fault is imposed directly on them. In the case of a presumption of fault model, it is not for the court to determine whether a person is at fault, but whether or not the defendant has brought sufficient evidence to show the absence of fault. Such a model of liability may, depending on the circumstances of the case, lead to a situation in which liability is imposed on a person who is not at fault for the damage alleged but who is simply unable to rebut the presumption because of the absence of evidence. For this reason, this pattern of liability is referred to in some sources of legal doctrine as 'quasi-strict liability'.[329] Under current regulation, the presumption of liability of the owner follows from the fact that it is upon the owner to prove that they have indeed given their animal to another person's supervision. The subsidiary liability obligation is applicable if the owner proves that the animal was transferred to another person at the time of occurrence of the damage, to which Article 2366 of the Civil Law indicates, i.e., the owner's liability occurs in the event that and to the extent that it is not possible to obtain compensation from the user or holder of the thing (animal).

328. Bitāns, A. (1997), *supra* n. 315, 128.lpp.
329. Torgāns, K., Kārkliņš, J., Bitāns, A. (2017), *supra* n. 70, 314.lpp.

# Part III. Forms of Strict Liability

## General Introduction

*172.* Dr Monika Hinteregger (Professor of the University of Graz, Austria) validly emphasizes that all European jurisdictions provide a sort of fault-based liability.[330] Latvia is no exception, with its general requirement of fault as one of the preconditions for liability as the consequence of a tort.[331] However, in certain categories, strict liability is applicable instead of a fault-based liability.

*173.* Dutch Professor Cees van Dam asserts that strict liability may be split into three types – liability with an extra debtor, liability for a defective object, and liability with limited defence.[332] Current Latvian tort law covers two of these variations. Distinguished Latvian legal scholar Professor Kalvis Torgāns opined that strict liability in Latvia is applicable in relatively narrow areas – liability for damage caused by a source of abnormal danger and product liability.[333] Bearing that in mind, the co-authors of this monograph conclude that Latvian tort law provides strict liability in the meaning of liability with limited defence and liability for a defective object. Latvian law does not provide liability with an extra debtor as strict liability. However, Latvian law provides joint and several liability[334] as well as noxal liability (an action brought against someone for damage or injury done by a person or animal belonging to them),[335] but does not consider them as strict liability.

*174.* In addition, one may argue that, in essence, strict liability with a limited defence is also stipulated if damage is caused by falling or accidentally dropped items (including liquids). A person who uses the part of a residential building from

330. Hinteregger, M. Economic Analysis of Law and Wilburg's Flexible System: A Systematic Approach to European Tort Law. The Shifting Meaning of Legal Certainty in Comparative and Transnational Law. Oxford and Portland, Oregon: Hart Publishing, 2017, p.100.
331. Article 1635 CL.
332. Van Dam, C. European Tort Law. Second Edition. Oxford: Oxford University Press, 2013, pp. 299, 301.
333. Torgāns, K.; Kārkliņš, J.; Bitāns, A. (2017), *supra* n. 70, 131.lpp.
334. Article 1670 CL.
335. Article 1782 CL.

which an item has fallen or been dropped is liable for damage caused. Legal scholars in the first part of the twentieth century asserted that such a user is liable, irrespective of whether they acted with fault or not.[336] This conclusion is upheld by the wording of the law, stipulating that this user may later claim compensation from the person at fault for the amount which they paid to the person to whom damage was caused.[337] As the law does not allow a person to whom damage is caused to claim compensation of damage from both the user of building and the person who actually caused the damage, this may not be considered as liability with an extra debtor. Another possible case of strict liability is the situation with the liability of a seller or provider of services, who is liable to a consumer for any defect in goods sold or services provided which existed at the moment of sale or provision.[338]

*175.* Product liability in Latvia is regulated in the same manner as throughout the entire EU on the basis of Directive 85/374/EEC.[339] The same conclusion, however, cannot be arrived at concerning liability for damage caused by a source of abnormal danger.

*176.* In general, the term 'source of abnormal danger' *(paaugstinātas bīstamības avots* in Latvian*)* used by the Civil Law is a synonym for the term 'abnormal dangerous activity' under Article 5:101 of the Principles of European Tort Law (the PETL). At first glance, it may seem self-evident that in this case the preconditions for application of this form of liability in Latvian law will be the same as provided by the PETL. However, it is not that simple.

*177.* The Civil Law explicitly provides several examples of a source of abnormal danger.[340] The law mentions transport (more precisely, use of transport), enterprise, construction, and dangerous substances. However, this list is not complete and these examples cause more confusion than clarity. The problem with them is twofold. First of all, depending on circumstances, each of these examples in one case may be considered as a source of abnormal danger, but not in another. [341] Second, the wording of these examples is rather broad and hence can include a huge subvariety of examples. For instance, the use of transport may include the use of a bicycle (which, of course, is highly unlikely to be considered as a source of abnormal danger) and may include the use of a dumper truck, which, of course, may involve a higher probability of risk and associated damage. Construction may mean small repairs in one's own private house or flat but may also mean the construction of a huge multi-storey building in the centre of an intensively occupied city. Dangerous substances may be included in some household chemicals, from which the

336. Буковскій, с. (1914), *supra* n. 150, с. 2023., Sinaiskis, V. (1996), *supra* n. 116, 234.lpp.
337. Article 2360 (1) CL.
338. Article 13 (2) Consumers Rights Protection Tenancy'. Official translation into English available at https://likumi.lv/ta/en/en/id/23309-consumer-rights-protection-law [accessed on 5 Mar. 2022]
339. Council Directive 85/374/EEC of 25 Jul. 1985 on the approximation of the laws, regulations and administrative provisions of the Member States concerning liability for defective products. OJ, L 210, 7 Aug. 1985, pp. 29–33.
340. Article 2347(2) CL.
341. Torgāns, K. (2018), *supra* n. 11, 479.lpp.

average person will not be able to extract them, unless they possess special skills and most likely also special equipment, in contrast to the case when these substances are stored somewhere in huge concentration. Therefore assessing whether a particular activity will be treated as a source of abnormal danger requires looking to see whether this activity involves the respective particularities, which, however, are the subject of discussion. The thin and often blurred line between sources of abnormal danger and other activities may also be seen in Latvian court practice regarding damage caused by road and traffic accidents.

## Chapter 1. Road and Traffic Accidents

*178.* One notable controversy in Latvian court practice on compensation of damage caused by road and traffic accidents concerns the issue of whether strict liability will be applied to all cases of traffic accidents, including situations when an accident is caused by the driver of a regular car, but not dumper trucks and other specialized vehicles. This question stems from the issue of whether driving a regular car is a matter of common usage.

*179.* Under Article 5:101(2) of the PETL, the activity should not be a matter of common usage in order to find it abnormally dangerous and to apply strict liability for damage that it causes. The Civil Law does not impose an explicit requirement for an activity not to be a matter of common usage and court practice varies in this respect.

*180.* In one judgment, the Supreme Court analysed the application of law in a situation regarding compensation of material and non-material damage caused by the severe consequences of a traffic accident.[342] The court found that the accident was caused by the driver of a vehicle which (according to publicly available information) requires a category B driver's licence,[343] i.e., the same as any vehicle for personal use. Hence it may be concluded that driving such a car may be considered a matter of common usage. However, in the given circumstances, the Supreme Court completely overlooked this aspect, which would logically lead to the conclusion that Article 2347(2) of the Civil Law is not applicable, as this case was not dealing with damage caused by a source of abnormal danger. Instead, the Supreme Court, in point 10.1 of the judgment, came to an excessively broad conclusion, namely that the owner of the vehicle, whose employee was the driver who caused the accident, was liable for all the damage caused by the accident, hence applying strict liability under the provision in question. After a year, the Supreme Court came to a rather opposite conclusion in another case.[344] Namely, in point 6 of its judgment, the Supreme Court found that Article 2347 of the Civil Law does not preclude holding the person who caused a traffic accident liable.[345] Hence the court preferred in that case to apply the fault-based liability model instead of the wide application of strict liability for damage caused by a source of abnormal danger.

*181.* Another characteristic aspect of liability for damage caused by motor vehicle drivers in road traffic is that this liability is subject to compulsory insurance. This requirement of compulsory insurance involves several particularities.

---

342. Judgment of the Supreme Court of 6 February 2013 in Case No. SKC-549/2013. Available at http://www.at.gov.lv/lv/tiesu-prakse/judikaturas-nolemumu-arhivs/tiesibu-aktu-raditajs [accessed on 3 May. 2021].
343. *See*, e.g.: https://busu-noma.lv/pakalpojums/renault-master-maxi/ [accessed on 3 May. 2021].
344. Judgment of the Supreme Court of 27 Nov. 2014 in Case No. SKC-156/2014. Available at http://www.at.gov.lv/lv/tiesu-prakse/judikaturas-nolemumu-arhivs/tiesibu-aktu-raditajs [accessed on 3 May. 2021].
345. *Ibid.*, point 6.

*182.* First of all, as in the case of any insurance contract, a motor insurance contract has a liability limit, i.e., the maximum amount of insurance indemnity to be provided by the motor insurer. Currently, the Motor Insurance Law sets a 5,210,000 EUR limit on the insurance indemnity for non-material damage to be covered in one insurance event irrespective of the number of injured persons and 1,050,000 EUR limit for material damage irrespective of the number of injured persons.[346] The Motor Insurance Law also lists certain types of damage, which are covered under compulsory insurance.[347] This might be considered as a somewhat misleading construction of the law, creating an impression that the Motor Insurance Law provides a special list for types of compensable damage, thus derogating from the types of damage stipulated in the Civil Law. Early Latvian court practice considered that these liability limits and types of damage covered do not mean that an injured person cannot claim the rest of the amount from the person liable.[348] The situation in this case was that the traffic accident involved a tractor which was transporting a poisonous chemical. In the result of the accident, the chemical flew into the soil, causing substantial pollution, removal of which required a large amount of work and also made drinking water unusable. The pollution also caused severe health problems to people living nearby. Last but not least, in the result of the accident, the tractor crashed into buildings, inflicting damage. The insurer paid the insurance indemnity; however, not all types of actual damage were covered by the indemnity, so that the injured persons claimed the rest of the damage from the owner of the tractor. The appeal instance court dismissed the claim, stating that the claimants had already received insurance indemnity covering the amount of damage where the applicable law requires insurance coverage. However, the Supreme Court quashed this judgment, finding that that approach was contrary to the very right of a fair trial. Injured persons may not undoubtedly claim from the insurer the types of damage not covered by an insurance policy, but this does not preclude them from claiming the rest of the damage from the person liable. In a more recent case, the Supreme Court emphasized that possibilities to claim the rest of the damage are subject to the assessment of fault. This remaining part of the damage may not be claimed if it appears that the defendant has not acted with fault, even if their insurer has earlier paid the insurance indemnity and thus covered part of the damage.[349]

*183.* Another interesting question was examined by the Supreme Court in a traffic accident case where bodily harm was caused to the injured person, and therefore, criminal proceedings were also commenced.[350] The person who caused the

346. Article 15(1) Compulsory Civil Liability Insurance of Owners of Motors Vehicles Law. Official translation into English available at https://likumi.lv/ta/en/en/id/87547-compulsory-civil-liability-insurance-of-owners-of-motor-vehicles-law [accessed on 5 May. 2022].

347. *Ibid.*, Art. 19 (1) (2).

348. Judgment of the Supreme Court of 21 Feb. 2013 in Case No. SKC-36/2013. Available at http://www.at.gov.lv/lv/tiesu-prakse/judikaturas-nolemumu-arhivs/tiesibu-aktu-raditajs [accessed on 3 Sep. 2021].

349. Judgment of the Supreme Court of 5 Mar. 2015 in Case No. SKC-250/2015. Not published.

350. Judgment of the Supreme Court of 17 Dec. 2020 in Case No. SKC-808/2020. Available at http://www.at.gov.lv/lv/tiesu-prakse/judikaturas-nolemumu-arhivs/tiesibu-aktu-raditajs [accessed on 3 Sep. 2021].

accident and who was accused in the criminal proceedings concluded a settlement with the injured person, under which the wrongdoer had compensated damage to the victim so that the victim, therefore, had no claims against the wrongdoer. However, the victim considered that not all of their damage was compensated by the wrongdoer and filed a claim against the insurance company. The appeal instance court satisfied the claim and the insurance company filed a cassation appeal. However, the Supreme Court upheld the judgment of the appeal instance court, finding that:

(1) the main purpose of compulsory insurance is to protect injured persons. Therefore all limitations to the rights of those persons to claim indemnity from the insurance company shall be interpreted narrowly;
(2) compensation of damage which the victim may claim from the wrongdoer during the course of criminal proceedings does not overlap with damage covered by compulsory insurance;
(3) the settlement was concluded between the wrongdoer and the victim and the insurance company was not a party to this settlement. Therefore this settlement may not affect the insurer's rights and obligations.

*184.* In certain cases, the Motor Insurance Law[351] provides the motor insurer with the possibility for a recourse claim in respect of the indemnity paid. Depending on the specific situation, a recourse claim may alternatively be filed against one of several persons, for instance, the owner or user of the vehicle involved. As specified by the Supreme Court, such a situation means that the indemnity paid may be recovered from one or another person, but not from both in a double or otherwise overlapping amount.[352]

*185.* In general, the owner or possessor (user) of a vehicle is responsible for the consequences of accidents caused by the use of the vehicle.[353] If these persons have negligently lost possession of the vehicle, liability for the damage will be split on a *culpa mixta* basis between the owner or possessor and actual user of the vehicle. However, in practice, the application of this provision is uncertain and extremely rare. The owner or possessor of the vehicle is not liable for damage if the accident was caused by force majeure or intent or gross negligence of the injured person. [354]

351. Article 41 Compulsory Civil Liability Insurance of Owners of Motors Vehicles Law. Official translation into English available at https://likumi.lv/ta/en/en/id/87547-compulsory-civil-liability-insurance-of-owners-of-motor-vehicles-law [accessed on 5 May. 2022].
352. Judgment of the Supreme Court of the Republic of Latvia of 25 Nov. 2013 in Case No. SKC-616/2013. Available at http://www.at.gov.lv/lv/tiesu-prakse/judikaturas-nolemumu-arhivs/tiesibu-akturaditajs [accessed on 3 Sep. 2021].
353. Article 44(2) Road Traffic Law.
354. Article 2347(2) first sentence CL.

## Chapter 2. Product Liability

*186.* As we have seen, product liability in Latvia (apart from liability for damage caused by a source of abnormal danger) is another example of application of strict liability. At the EU level, regulation of product liability is based on Directive 85/374/EEC, the Product Liability Directive,[355] which Professor Cees van Dam called the oldest and still most powerful example of European harmonization in the field of tort law.[356] At the national level, this directive is implemented in Latvian national law by the Law 'On Liability for Defects of Goods and Services' *(Likums par atbildību par preces un pakalpojuma trūkumiem* in Latvian; Product Liability Law).[357] Professor van Dam also mentions that the Product Liability Directive harmonizes product liability only to a certain extent, so that substantial differences remain between liability regimes in different EU Member States.[358] Professor van Dam also emphasizes that the Directive provided two options for the EU Member States to derogate to some extent from it. Historically there was also the third option: to rule that manufacturers of raw agricultural products and game would not fall under the scope of the directive. This, however, was abolished in 2000. The first of the two existing options is the possibility to exclude the so-called development risk defence. This defence is provided in Article 7 (e) of the Product Liability Directive, which states that a producer of goods will not be liable if they prove that the state of scientific and technical knowledge at the time when they put the product into circulation was not such as to enable the existence of the defect to be discovered.[359] Latvia has not derogated from this provision as it is included in Article 13(1)(4) of the Product Liability Law, in exactly the same wording as in the Directive itself. The second option is to limit producers' total liability for damage resulting from the death or personal injury and caused by identical items with the same defect in an amount not less than 70 million ECU (i.e., 70 million EUR).[360] This option is not used by Latvia either.

*187.* Applying product liability necessarily involves a defective product which has caused damage and which has been sold or provided (offered) to consumers. Article 3 of the Product Liability Law defines a product as a movable tangible thing, including gas and electricity, as well as services. Under Article 7(1) of the Product Liability Law, a product is defective if it does not provide the safety which a person is entitled to expect, taking all circumstances into account. However, this provision, which is directly borrowed from the Product Liability Directive, requires some clarification. Professor van Dam observes that in practice a distinction is usually drawn between manufacturing defects, on the one hand, and design and instruction

355. Council Directive 85/374/EEC of 25 Jul. 1985 on the approximation of the laws, regulations and administrative provisions of the Member States concerning liability for defective products. OJ, L 210, 7.8.1985, pp. 29–33.
356. Van Dam, C. (2013), *supra* n. 332, p. 420.
357. *Ibid.*
358. *Ibid.*
359. *Ibid.*, p. 423.
360. *Ibid.*, p. 424.

defects, on the other.[361] Product liability ensures the right to claim damage basically in cases where a defect is caused by shortcomings during manufacture. In the case of design and instruction defects, compensation of damage is subject to several preconditions,[362] which in the case of Latvian law are the same as in the Directive and are provided in bullet points 1 - 4 of Article 7(1) Product Liability Law.

*188.* First, a description of the goods – their structure and packaging will be taken into account. Second, the instructions (manuals) for installation or use will be taken into account. This aspect requires a producer to properly instruct the consumer on how to use and employ the product. This includes appropriate warnings about safety measures and precautions, especially when, for instance, a product is some sort of household chemical, also information about possible side effects, which is especially relevant in the case of various medical/medicinal products.

*189.* Third, the use of the goods under normal or expected circumstances will be taken into account. As Professor van Dam puts it – what type of (negligent) use might the producer expect from the customer? This includes the assumption that customers make mistakes and do not always use a product in a safe or even in a proper way. For instance, children may try to put toys in their mouth or even swallow them. Therefore the producer must take this into account and make the product safer or, when this is not reasonably feasible, provide effective warnings to the customer.[363]

*190.* Fourth, the time when the product was put into circulation will be taken into account. Thus, if later safer and better products are created and put into circulation, this does not *per se* mean that earlier products are defective.

*191.* These rather extensive provisions, however, do not mean that there are no situations in Latvian court practice when serious discussion could arise as to whether product liability was applied properly, i.e., in a situation dealing with damage caused by a *defective product sold or provided to a consumer.*

*192.* One such example is a judgment of the appeal instance court where the court applied product liability to the operator of a supermarket in a situation where a metal shelf with goods stored on it fell upon someone visiting the shop with the purpose of buying goods, causing severe injuries which also led to the victim suffering from mental issues.[364] It is not fully clear from the text of judgment itself why the shelf fell, i.e., because it was not properly fixed or for some other reason. Nevertheless, the court applied product liability in order to adjudicate the case.

361. *Ibid.*, p. 428
362. *Ibid.*
363. *Ibid.*, p. 429.
364. Judgment of Zemgale Regional Court of 19 Nov. 2020 in Case No C16076617. Not published.

*193.* There is no doubt that someone in such a situation, as discussed in the previous paragraph should be entitled to receive full compensation for damage. However, the question is whether a shelf, which is not a product offered to customers, should be considered as a product within the meaning of product liability. Even if the answer is affirmative, how is it possible to apply product liability without stating that a product was defective? Such questions raise concerns, perhaps for other justifications for the imposition of liability, for instance, whether liability for maintaining a public place (supermarket) in a safe condition, which under Latvian law is subject to fault-based liability, would be more appropriate.

*194.* A similar inappropriate application of product liability could be found in another case involving closing of doors. In this case, the sensors of the automatic doors in a supermarket were not properly adjusted and as a result the doors started to close when the claimant was going through the doorway, pushing the claimant, who fell to the floor and was injured.[365] Although in this case the claimant most likely should be entitled to compensation, product liability should not be seen as the correct ground for claim because neither the doors nor the sensors were products offered to consumers. Most likely liability should be applied to the entity that owes a duty to ensure the proper functioning of the doors and the ground for liability could then be general provisions for negligence. Latvian court practice also features more examples when product liability has been applied in similar – highly disputable, to say the least – situations.[366]

*195.* Another less contradictory, but still discussable, example of application of product liability can be found in a case concerning a slippery floor in a hotel bathroom. In this case, the claimant was staying at a hotel, where she slipped on the bathroom floor, where water was left, and thus received quite severe injuries. This situation might be treated as improper provision of hotel services which led to personal injury.[367] However, the court interestingly finds in the judgment that the water was left due to the negligence of the hotel.[368] If so, then application of product liability, and strict liability stemming therefrom, has no real necessity because the case may be properly adjudicated on the basis of general liability for negligence.

*196.* However, it would be wrong to conclude that Latvian courts are applying product liability inappropriately in most cases. Instead, there are several plausible examples in Latvian court practice as well.

*197.* One particular case involved a dispute over use of a house heating system. The owner of a family house concluded a contract with the defendant, who undertook to build a heating system in the claimant's house. The heating system was installed but did not function properly. Moreover, it inflicted damage on several structures of the house due to overheating and other similar factors. The dispute in

365. Judgment of Latgale Regional Court of 4 Apr. 2019 in Case No. C12253717. Not published.
366. Judgment of Kurzeme Regional Court of 22 Jun. 2017 in Case No. C20253716. Not published.
367. Judgment of Riga Regional Court of 23 Feb. 2021 in Case No. C30852919. Not published.
368. *Ibid*, p. 3.

the case was whether the claimant had used the system properly. However, in those circumstances, the court validly emphasized that, among other aspects, the defendant had not provided the claimant with instructions for the use of the system. This means that the product in any case had a substantial instruction-related defect, namely, the absence of instruction.[369]

*198.* The defences available in the Product Liability Law are precisely the same as provided in the Product Liability Directive. Namely, under Article 13 of the Product Liability Law, a manufacturer will not be liable if it proves that:

(1) it has not put the goods into circulation;
(2) taking into account the relevant circumstances, there is reason to believe that the defect which caused the damage appeared after the goods were put into circulation;
(3) the goods were not manufactured for putting into circulation or for other forms of distribution for the purpose of making a profit, nor were they manufactured or distributed within the scope of economic activities;
(4) the level of scientific and technological development at the time when the goods were put into circulation was not so high as to enable the defect or flaw to be discovered;
(5) the defect in the goods resulted from the fact that the manufacturer complied with requirements set by the state or local government.

*199.* In turn, a service provider will not be liable if it proves that:

(1) taking into account the relevant circumstances, there is reason to believe that the defect which caused the damage appeared after the provision of the service;
(2) the level of scientific and technological development at the time when the services were provided was not so high as to enable the defect to be discovered;
(3) the defect in services resulted from the fact that the service provider complied with requirements set by the state or local government.

*200.* The manufacturer of a component will not be liable if it proves that a defect of goods or services is related to the structure of the goods or the property in which the component has been placed (fitted) or to the instructions (manuals) given by the manufacturer of the goods or the service provider.[370]

*201.* As appears from the wording of Article 13 of the Product Liability Law, the *onus probandi* for proving these defences is imposed on the manufacturer or service provider. Perhaps, for this reason, these defences are not widely used and hence are not also widely analysed in Latvian court practice. However, there is one other

369. Judgment of Latgale Regional Court from 24 Apr. 2017 in Case No.C39074309. Not published.
370. Article 13 (3) Product Liability Law. Official translation into English available at https://likumi.lv/ta/en/en/id/8683-on-liability-for-defects-of-goods-and-services [accessed on 5 May. 2022].

interesting example of a defence which, although not successful, is worth a mention. The dispute was between the owner of a family house (claimant) and a supplier of electricity (defendant). One day electricity supplied to the house suffered several cuts, which caused damage to several items of household equipment. The defendant supplier of electricity pointed out that the claimant had not installed in their house the equipment which could have prevented damage from an electricity cut. Hence, in the view of the defendant, the damage was caused with contributory fault by the injured person, which, under Article 12 of the Product Liability Law, may be a reason to wholly release the defendant from liability. However, in the given circumstances, the court dismissed that argument, stating that the damage was inflicted on household equipment whose use does not require installation of said equipment for minimizing the consequences of electricity supply cuts.[371]

*202.* As product liability is based on the strict liability model, this means that the claimant has no need to prove intent or negligence on the part of the producer of goods or provider of services. However, the claimant is still required to prove the defect in a product, damage, and causality between the defect and the damage caused. Indeed, the requirement to prove the existence of these preconditions may amount to a substantive issue, which may determine the outcome of the case. Such a situation occurred in a case where a water leak from a washing machine caused damage to the owner of the flat where the machine was located and used, and by other neighbouring flats. The court emphasized that in order to apply product liability, the claimant has to prove the product defect and said causality, which, in the given case the claimant had not done because they considered the necessary expertise to be too expensive.[372] Professor van Dam argues that in the case of product liability, the court may find the existence of defect and causality on the basis of *res ipsa loquitur*, providing that the court may find these preconditions in a situation when the facts give reason to believe (i.e., prima facie evidence) that the product was defective and caused the damage, for example, if a television catches fire because of a short circuit.[373] Perhaps such an approach might have changed the result in the above-mentioned case; however, it was not applied.

*203.* Similarly to Article 10 of the Product Liability Directive, Article 14 of the Product Liability Law provides two limitation periods for a claim. The first term with a length of three years starts at the moment when the injured person became aware or should have reasonably have been aware of the damage, the defect, and the identity of the producer. The second term expires after ten years from the date when the producer puts into circulation the actual product which caused the damage. This detail proved to be important in a case reviewed by an appeal instance court.[374] In this case, the claimant bought a TV in 2008 but a couple of months later

371. Judgment of Riga City Ziemelu District Court of 24 Apr. 2017 in Case No. C32297415. Not published.
372. Judgment of Zemgale Regional Court of 2 Nov. 2017 in Case No. C33253315. Not published.
373. Van Dam, C. (2013), *supra* n. 332, p. 438.
374. Judgment of Riga Regional Court of 10 Jul. 2020 in Case No. C30553216 (archive No.CA-0532-20/26).

electrical issues in the TV caused a fire incident in the claimant's flat. As the claimant was not aware of the producer of the TV, they sued the shop from whom they bought the TV. In 2013 the shop submitted a letter to the court informing the claimant about the producer of the TV. Nevertheless, the litigation continued and ended with a settlement between the claimant and the shop owner, according to which the shop owner paid compensation to the claimant. However, later the claimant filed a new claim against the producer of the TV, but both the first instance court and also an appeal instance court dismissed the claim stating that the limitation period had expired. If the claimant was informed about the producer and was already aware of the damage and the defect, then the three-year limitation period should be applied and should commence right from the moment when the claimant was informed about all these three aspects. However, these aspects, as emphasized by the appeal instance court, do not determine the starting point of the ten-year limitation period. This period starts from the moment when the product is put into circulation by the producer. Moreover, the ten-year limitation period should not be applied if the three-year period is applicable.[375]

375. *Ibid.*

## Chapter 3. Liability for Services

*204.* The Civil Law does not provide a strict liability model for services. However, in this context, the strict liability model for construction and enterprise as potential sources of abnormal danger may come into play.

*205.* Latvian court practice does not have a substantial amount of cases when damage is caused by operation of an enterprise. However, not every enterprise will be treated as a source of abnormal danger,[376] but rather one whose operation creates a risk of danger which cannot be eliminated even by exercising due care.

*206.* If damage is caused as a result of construction, a specific construction regulation is often applied. In a particular case, the Supreme Court analysed the distribution of liability between the owner of a building (tower) crane and its lessee, who was at the same time also the lessee of the real estate where the crane was used for construction works and caused damage. The court emphasized that although the owner of the crane may be considered as its possessor, the lessee of the crane exercised actual control over operations with the crane and was entitled to give binding instructions to the operator of the crane. Hence it may be concluded that the person liable – the performer of abnormally dangerous activities – is the one who exercises actual control over those activities and therefore is in the best position to evaluate the possible risks and prevent damage.[377]

376. Torgāns, K. (2018), *supra* n. 11, 479.lpp.
377. Judgment of the Supreme Court of 20 Jan. 2020 in Case No. SKC-51/2020. Available at http://www.at.gov.lv/lv/tiesu-prakse/judikaturas-nolemumu-arhivs/tiesibu-aktu-raditajs [accessed on 26 Jun. 2021].

## Chapter 4. Environmental Liability

*207.* As an EU Member State, Latvia has implemented Directive 2004/35/CE[378] in the Environment Protection Law *(Vides aizsardzības likums* in Latvian*)*.[379] The Directive does not explicitly require the EU Member States to apply strict liability regarding compensation of damage caused to environmental resources. However, similarly to Germany,[380] the Civil Law does not impose the strict liability model in some (although not all) cases involving compensation for damage to the environment. The general principle of law is that an operator who carries out an activity which may cause pollution or otherwise cause environmental damage is liable for intentional or negligent breach of legal provisions concerning the protection of the environment.[381] Yet in certain cases the operator may face strict liability under a liability model irrespective of intent or negligence on the part of a tortfeasor. The following cases are explicitly envisaged in law dealing with certain activities, i.e.:

- polluting activities of Category A or B that are laid down in the law On Pollution (for example, operation of installations for metal ore, including sulphide ore, roasting and sintering; or operation of installations for the production of asbestos and the manufacture of asbestos-based products);
- activities for the performance of which a waste management permit is required;
- water abstraction and impoundment where a water resources use permit is required;
- operation of a filling station or petroleum storage facility;
- manufacture, use, processing, packaging, distribution into the environment or movement within the territory of the production unit of hazardous chemical substances or products (preparations), plant protection products or also biocides specified under laws and regulations (regulating the circulation of chemical substances and mixtures);
- transportation of chemical substances or mixtures through pipelines;
- transportation of dangerous or polluting cargoes by land, inland waters, sea or air;
- limited use, deliberate distribution into the environment, placing on the market, also the movement of genetically modified organisms, also genetically modified micro-organisms;
- transboundary movement of waste specified in regulations of the European Union for the performance of which a permit is required;
- management of extractive industry waste.[382]

---

378. Directive 2004/35/CE of the European Parliament and of the Council of 21 Apr. 2004 on environmental liability with regard to the prevention and remedying of environmental damage. OJ, L 143, 30 Apr. 2004, pp. 56–75.
379. Environment Protection Law. Official translation into English available on the official web-page of the State Language Centre at https://vvc.gov.lv/image/catalog/dokumenti/Environmental%20Protection%20Law.docx [accessed on 26 Jun. 2021].
380. Van Dam, C. (2013), *supra* n. 332, p. 442.
381. Article 25(1) Environmental Protection Law. Official translation into English available at https://likumi.lv/ta/en/en/id/147917-environmental-protection-law [accessed on 05 Mar. 2022].
382. *Ibid.*, Art. 25(4).

*208.* Irrespective of whether a particular case is based on the strict liability or fault-based liability model, the law does not provide that causation between the activities of a particular operator and environmental damage could be presumed or even established on a *res ipsa loquitur* basis: causation still needs to be proved. Under the law, the State Environmental Service (*Valsts vides dienests* in Latvian) is required to identify the operator whose occupational activities caused damage to the environment and to adopt a decision accordingly.[383] This decision may be contested before the State Environmental Supervision Bureau (*Vides pārraudzības valsts birojs* in Latvian) within fifteen days and the decision of State Environmental Supervision Bureau may subsequently be contested before the administrative court.[384] However, as always, the devil is in the details. In this case, the important detail is that the decision of State Environmental Service identifying the operator whose occupational activities caused damage to the environment may be adopted either separately or together with the decision on immediate or sanitary measures to be taken. In this context, the Supreme Court found that the operator is entitled to dispute the decision identifying the operator, even if a decision on measures is not taken. However, if a decision on measures is taken together with the decision on identification of the operator or soon after, the operator is not entitled to dispute the decision on identifying the operator separately, but only the decision on measures.[385]

*209.* Even in the case of imposition of the strict liability model for environmental damage, the operator is entitled to certain defences, releasing them from liability. Liability is not applicable if damage occurred due to a natural phenomenon of exceptional, inevitable, unpredictable in due time and irresistible character or due to armed conflict, hostilities, civil war or insurrection. There are also no grounds for liability for environmental damage caused by activities whose principal aim is national defence or international security, as well as environmental damage caused by activities whose only aim is protection from natural disaster.[386]

383. *Ibid.*, Art. 28(1).
384. *Ibid.*, Art. 28(5).
385. Decision of the Supreme Court of 28 Apr. 2020 in Case No. SKA-964/2020. Available at http://www.at.gov.lv/lv/tiesu-prakse/judikaturas-nolemumu-arhivs/tiesibu-aktu-raditajs [accessed on 1 Oct. 2021].
386. Article 35(1) and (2) Environmental Protection Law, *supra* n. 380.

## Chapter 5. Other

*210.* Apart from Article 2347(2) of the Civil Law and other provisions imposing strict liability already mentioned above, Latvian law establishes several other cases, when the strict liability model might be applicable. However, as Professor Kārkliņš has validly emphasized, these cases are highly controversial, especially regarding the question of whether the given cases are cases of strict liability or fault-based liability.[387]

*211.* One case involving this controversy, mentioned by Kārkliņš, is related to a rail carrier's liability and stems from the following wording of the law:

> A carrier shall be liable for damage caused as a result of an act (omission) of the carrier during carriage, if a passenger has died or has become crippled or has incurred other damage to health, or the property of passengers has been damaged and the carrier cannot prove that the damage has been caused due to force majeure, with the intention of the injured person himself or herself, or due to his or her gross negligence.[388] A carrier shall be liable for damage caused during boarding and alighting of passengers if the carrier is determined to be at fault.

On the one hand, the construction of this provision seems to be similar to a provision imposing strict liability. On the other hand, the statement that a carrier is liable for an act (omission) is not typical of the strict liability model. As a result, this provision rather looks like imposing fault-based liability.[389] This question has not so far been settled in Latvian court practice.

*212.* Obvious imposition of strict liability is provided in the Law on Carriage by Road (*Autopārvadājumu likums* in Latvian).[390] This Law provides that a carrier is liable for damage caused in the course of carriage if a passenger has died, has suffered bodily injury or damage to their property has been caused and the carrier fails to prove that the damage was incurred due to force majeure, with the intention of the victim in person, or due to the gross negligence of the victim.[391] This provision clearly stipulates liability irrespective of fault, as well as an exhaustive list of defences and the duty to prove any of those defences that a carrier relies on. However, the second sentence of this provision also stipulates that a carrier is liable for

---

387. Kārkliņš, J. Stingrās atbildības izslēdzošie apstākļi [*Exceptions of Strict Liability*]. Ārvalsts investīcijas: kad tiesības mijiedarbojas. Latvijas Universitātes 74. zinātniskās konferences rakstu krājums. Rīga: LU Akademiskais apgāds, 2016, 124–125.lpp.
388. Article 54 Rail Carriage Law. Official translation into English available on the official web-page of the State Language Centre at https://vvc.gov.lv/image/catalog/dokumenti/Carriage%20by%20Rail.docx[accessed on 15 Jan. 2022].
389. Kārkliņš, J. (2016), *supra* n. 387, 124.lpp.
390. Law on Carriage by Road. Official translation into English available on the official web-page of the State Language Centre at https://vvc.gov.lv/image/catalog/dokumenti/Law%20on%20Carriage%20by%20Road.docx [accessed on 15 Jan. 2022].
391. Article 40(6) Law on Carriage by Road.

damage caused during embarkation or disembarkation of passengers and loading or unloading of luggage if the carrier has acted with fault (i.e., fault-based liability).[392] In this context, Kārkliņš criticized a judgment of the Supreme Court[393] where the Court concluded that the law provides strict liability only for material damage inflicted on a passenger during transportation. But, as the Supreme Court established, if the carrier also inflicted personal damage, compensation will be attributed according to fault-based liability. It is worth mentioning that this statement was made on the basis of Article 2347(1) and (2) of the Civil Law, which provides at least grammatical grounds for such interpretation. Moreover, the Supreme Court has also provided rather extensive clarification on why that interpretation should be considered as intended by the legislator. Therefore, it should be viewed as a clear intention of the lawmaker, not a mere interpretation by the court. Kārkliņš criticizes this approach by the court for applying two different liability regimes for one potential case when the victim has faced material as well as personal damage.[394] Of course, opinions on this matter may differ. However, this restrictive interpretation by the Supreme Court conforms to the limited nature of strict liability in Latvian law. It is also worth mentioning that the Supreme Court affirmed the same approach in another case reviewed in 2016.[395]

*213.* Another example of the strict liability model may be found in Article 79(1) of the Maritime Code, which applies strict liability to the owner of a ship for pollution by oil products. Articles 96 and 98 of the Law on Aviation lay down strict liability for the owner of an aircraft or flight operator for the death and bodily injury of a crew member or passenger, but Article 97 of the same law provides strict liability for the owner of an aircraft or flight operator if personal or material damage is caused to a third party by an aircraft in flight or an item separated from the aircraft.

392. Article 40(6) second sentence Law on Carriage by Road.
393. Judgment of the Supreme Court of 5 Mar. 2015 in Case No. SKC-250/2015. Not published.
394. Kārkliņš, J. (2016), *supra* n. 386, 124–125.lpp.
395. Judgment of the Supreme Court of 3 Jun. 2016 in Case No. SKC-143/2016. Not published.

# Part IV. Defences and Exception Clauses

## Chapter 1. Limitation of Action

*214.* The Civil Law sets a general limitation period of ten years.[396] As observed by Professor Vladimir Bukovsky at the beginning of the twentieth century, the general limitation period of ten years refers not only to various claims arising from the law of obligations but also from other branches of civil law, hence covering property law, inheritance law, family law, and so on, unless the law explicitly provides otherwise.[397]

*215.* Unlike German law, Latvian law does not distinguish between a relative and absolute limitation period except for the ten-year limitation period set in Article 14 of the Product Liability Law.[398] The consequence of expiry of the limitation period is essential termination of the respective claim.[399] Ten years is a rather long term. Therefore, it is no surprise that Latvian law provides numerous exceptions from the general limitation period. These are treated as special limitation periods. The following special limitation periods were introduced recently.

*216.* In the case of some quasi-torts, for example, if damage is caused by something being thrown or poured into the street or other place where people are walking or standing, or by inadequately fastened objects falling from a house onto the street, the limitation period for claiming damage is one year from the moment the damage occurred.[400]

*217.* A claim against a person who has unlawfully acquired, used or disclosed a trade secret may be brought within a limitation period of three years, starting from the moment when the trade secret holder becomes aware or should have become

396. Article 1895 CL.
397. Буковскій, В. (1914), *supra* n. 150, c. 1523.
398. Spindler, G., Rieckers, O. *Tort Law in Germany*. Third ed. AH Alphen aan den Rijn: Kluwer Law International, 2019, p.99.
399. Article 1893 CL.
400. Article 2362 CL.

aware of unlawful acquisition, use or disclosure of the trade secret.[401] This limitation applies to cases where a trade secret has been violated because of tort as well as where it was violated because of breach of contract.[402]

*218.* Although more related to contract law than tort law, a claim arising from commercial transactions, i.e., when at least one of the parties is a merchant, expires within a period of three years.[403] This means that a claim for compensation of damage caused by the breach of a commercial transaction will expire within a period of three years. Moreover, settled court practice suggests that the three-year limitation period set for claims arising from commercial transactions will also apply to quasi-contractual claims, where the payment obligation is set by law, for instance, the obligation of owners of residential buildings built during the Soviet period to pay rent to the owners of land plots under the residential building where they live.[404]

*219.* A claim for compensation of damage against the members of company supervisory and management boards expires within a five-year limitation period, running from the moment the damage is caused.[405] Regarding possible infringements committed by members of company supervisory and management boards, the question arises whether these infringements are attributable to the category of tort or to the category of quasi-contract. Some may validly point out that such a claim may be based merely on grounds stemming from law and imposing certain duties of board members on companies, such as the duty of loyalty to the company[406] and hence should be considered as a claim in tort. At the same time, it should not be ignored that some similarities could be seen between these infringements and infringements committed by the agent vis-à-vis principal. Therefore it may be said that an infringement committed by members of company supervisory and management boards causes a breach of a quasi-contractual obligation, although this obligation is not attributed to the list of 'classic quasi contracts', including unauthorized management of affairs *(negatorium gestio)*, *condictio* and unjust enrichment.[407]

*220.* Claims arising out of an insurance contract are statutorily limited to a period of three years.[408] A similar limitation period is set for claims arising from a

---

401. Article 7 Trade Secret Protection Law. Law on Carriage by Road. Official translation into English available on the official web-page of the State Language Centre at https://vvc.gov.lv/image/catalog/dokumenti/Trade%20Secret%20Protection%20Law.docx [accessed on 17 Jan. 2022].
402. *Ibid.*, Art. 5(1).
403. Article 406 KCL.
404. Judgment of 30 May. 2019 in Case No. SKC-104/2019. Available at https://www.at.gov.lv/lv/tiesu-prakse/judikaturas-nolemumu-arhivs/civillietu-departaments/hronologiska-seciba?lawfilter=0&year=2019 [accessed on 30 Oct. 2021].
405. Article 169(5) KCL.
406. Strupišs, A. *supra* n. 209.
407. Nicholas, B. An Introduction to Roman Law. Oxford: Oxford University Press, 2008, pp. 227–233.
408. Article 39 Insurance Contract Law. Official translation into English available on the official web-page of the State Language Centre at https://vvc.gov.lv/image/catalog/dokumenti/Insurance%20Contract%20Law.doc.

motor insurance contract.[409] In other words, a limitation period of the same length applies to claims by persons who are parties to an insurance contract (i.e., to claims arising from contractual liability) as well as to claims by third parties, such as persons injured or whose property was damaged as the result of use of a vehicle under motor insurance. Note that the Latvian legislator has recently substantially reduced the limitation period for filing a claim for insurance redress regarding an insured event dealing with a person's death or civil liability, as in such cases the limitation period was previously ten years, which was also confirmed in court practice.[410]

*221.* As we have seen, in the case of product liability, the law sets two different limitation periods for a claim.[411] A three-year limitation starts at the moment when an injured person became aware or should have reasonably have been aware, of the damage, the defect, and the identity of the producer. A ten-year limitation starts to run from the date when a producer puts into circulation the actual product that caused the damage.

*222.* General regulation of limitation periods prescribes that a limitation period starts to run at the moment when a claimant (creditor) is legally able to raise a claim against the defendant (debtor). This requires neither refusal by the debtor or a reminder from the creditor. However, if performance is subject to preconditions, these have to appear in order to make a limitation period start to run, and if a specific time was set for performance, this time must have passed.[412] Time limitations may be interrupted either by a simple reminder to the debtor or by filing a claim in court or arbitration.[413] Unless provisions stipulating a particular limitation period provide otherwise, the general provisions regarding interruption of the limitation period will also apply regarding interruption of the special limitation period. However, once the limitation period is interrupted, a new one begins under applicable special provisions.[414]

*223.* Special provisions are set for the commencement and interruption of a limitation period in cases regarding compensation of damage caused by a violation of competition law. The moment when the limitation period starts to run depends on the moment when the injured person was aware or should have been aware of three aspects:

---

409. Article 39(4$^1$) Compulsory Civil Liability Insurance of Owners of Motor Vehicles Law [Motor Insurance Law]. Official translation into English available on the official web-page of the State Language Centre at https://vvc.gov.lv/image/catalog/dokumenti/Compulsory%20Civil%20Liability%20Insurance%20of%20Owners%20of%20Motor%20Vehicles%20Law.docx.
410. Judgment of the Supreme Court of 12 Mar. 2014 in Case No. SKC-184/2014. Available at https://www.at.gov.lv/lv/tiesu-prakse/judikaturas-nolemumu-arhivs/civillietu-departaments/hronologiska-seciba?lawfilter=0&year=2014 [accessed on 30 Oct. 2021].
411. Article 14 Law on Liability for the Defects of Goods and Services.
412. Article 1896 CL.
413. Articles 1902 and 1905 CL.
414. Judgment of the Supreme Court of 14 Dec. 2017 in Case No. SKC-265/2017. Available at https://www.at.gov.lv/lv/tiesu-prakse/judikaturas-nolemumu-arhivs/civillietu-departaments/hronologiska-seciba?lawfilter=0&year=2017 [accessed on 30 Oct.2021].

(1) the behaviour and the fact that it constitutes an infringement of competition law;
(2) the fact that the infringement of competition law caused them harm; and
(3) the identity of the infringer.[415]

In this category of cases, the running of the limitation period is suspended for the period when the competition authority examines the case about a potential violation of competition law, as well as for the period when the decision of the competition authority is disputed in court.[416] These provisions implement EU law.[417]

*224.* Following the tradition of the Germanic legal system of the nineteenth century, Latvian law still differentiates between two types of deadline: the period limiting the action (*noilgums* in Latvian) and the period terminating a subjective right as such (*prekluzīvais termiņš* in Latvian or *Ausschlussfrist* in German). The main difference between these deadlines is that the expiry of the deadline limiting the action prevents enforcement of the obligation via court proceedings, but a debtor who for any reason performs the obligation after the expiry of the deadline is not entitled to reclaim performance, i.e., the law considers the obligation as still valid.[418] However, if the deadline terminating a subjective right as such has expired, it means that there is no corresponding obligation at all. Moreover, the court may ex officio examine the possible expiry of this deadline, while examination of possible expiry of the deadline limiting the action is allowed only where a party advances that argument.[419] However, the line between both types of deadline is often blurred. This unclear situation triggered a discussion in the first part of the twentieth century[420] that continues to this day. For example, various authors have discussed the three-month deadline for minority shareholders to file a claim against company founders, supervisory and management board members as well as auditors for compensation of damage caused to the company if the general meeting of the company shareholders has refused to bring an action or the general meeting was not convened in order to examine the issue of bringing a claim.[421] Initially, the opinion was that this deadline should be perceived as a limitation of action.[422] Later different opinion was provided, maintaining that it is the deadline terminating the

415. Article 21.[4] (1) Competition Law. Official translation into English available at https://likumi.lv/ta/en/en/id/54890-competition-law [accessed on 5 Mar. 2022].
416. *Ibid.*, Art. 21.[4] (2).
417. Directive 2014/104/EU of the European Parliament and of the Council of 26 Nov. 2014 on certain rules governing actions for damages under national law for infringements of the competition law provisions of the Member States and of the European Union. OJ, L 349, 5 Dec. 2014, pp. 1–19.
418. Article 1911 CL.
419. Bukovskis, V. Civīlprocesa mācības grāmata *[Textbook of Civil Procedure]*. Rīga: Autora izdevums, 1933, 278–279.lpp.
420. Lēbers, A. Par preklusiviem termiņiem *[On preclusive Time Limitations]*. Tieslietu Ministrijas Vēstnesis, Nr.1, 1 Jan. 1924.
421. Article 172 (6) KCL.
422. Strupišs, A. Komentārs Komerclikuma 172.pantam [*Commentary to Art. 172 of the Commercial Law*]. Komerclikuma komentāri III. B daļa. Komersanti. XI sadaļa. Kapitālsabiedrības (134–184. panti). Rīga: 'A. Strupiša juridiskais birojs' SIA, 2003, 168.lpp.

rights as such.[423] Recently several other authors asserted that it is just a deadline envisaged in law in order to discipline those who should proceed with bringing a claim.[424]

423. Rasnačs, L. Sabiedrības prasību celšana pēc mazākuma pieprasījuma [*Claims by a Company at the Request of a Minority*]. Jurista Vārds, 18 Sep. 2012; Judgment of the Supreme Court of 20 May 2016 in Case No. SKC-190/2016. Available at https://www.at.gov.lv/lv/tiesu-prakse/judikaturas-nolemumu-arhivs/civillietu-departaments/hronologiska-seciba?lawfilter=0&year=20176 (accessed on 18 Jan. 2022.); Strupišs A. Komentārs Komerclikuma 172.pantam [*Commentary to Article 172 of the Commercial Law*], 2019. Available at https://komentari.info/index.php?lv=1&likums=4&komentars=170 [accessed 30 Aug. 2021].

424. Rudāns, S. Valdes locekļa atbildība par sabiedrībai nodarītajiem zaudējumiem *[Liability of a Member of the Management Board for Damage Caused to a Company]*. Komerctiesību aktuālie jautājumi Latvijā un Eiropā. Komercdarījumi. Atbildība. Komercstrīdi. Rīga: Tiesu Namu Aģentūra, 2013, 227.lpp.; Kārkliņš, J., Brants, E. Par Komerclikuma 172. panta sestajā daļā noteiktā trīs mēnešu termiņa juridisko dabu. *[On the Legal Nature of the Three-month Time Limitation Stipulated in Article 172 (6) of the Commercial Law]* Jurista Vārds, 27 Oct. 2020., Nr. 43, 17.lpp.; Novicāne, E. Turpinot diskusiju par Komerclikuma 172. panta sestajā daļā noteiktā termiņa juridisko dabu. *[Continuing on the Legal Nature of the Three-month time Limitation Stipulated in Article 172 (6) of the Commercial Law]* Jurista Vārds, 10.11.2020., Nr. 45, 31.lpp.

# Chapter 2. Grounds of Justification

## §1. Consent

*225.* The law provides that there is no infringement if someone exercises their rights, is acting in line with the will of the injured person, or has to act in self-defence because of an illegal action by the injured person.[425] Hence this provision implements the principle *volenti non fit iniuria*, meaning that if someone is injured by their own consent, their injury may not be treated as a violation entitling the injured person to claim a remedy.[426]

*226.* Under Latvian legal doctrine, this provision may be relevant in two categories of cases:

(1) when someone willingly accepts injury (for instance, in the course of surgery), or
(2) when someone willingly accepts the risk of injury (for example, through participating in sporting activities that carry a substantial risk of injury or through the choice of profession that inevitably involves a substantial risk of injury (soldiers, police, firefighters)).[427] In both cases, it is important that consent is given willingly and seriously, i.e., without mistake or other defect of consent.[428]

*227.* However, it is also important to distinguish whether the injury was caused by the chosen activity alone or whether fault on the part of the defendant contributed to the injury. In addition, it is important to evaluate to what extent the activity involves the risk of injury because, once the risks are *per se* higher, the potential role of contributory fault is smaller. This distinction may be illustrated by examples from settled court practice.

*228.* The Supreme Court examined a case where a claim was brought against an ice-hockey coach, an ice-hockey club and the state in the person of the state agency responsible for supervising monitoring the health of athletes.[429] The facts of the case were that the person, who at that time was under the legal age, collapsed during ice-hockey training, even experienced clinical death and later had to undergo serious medical treatment and faced substantial damage to his health for the rest of his life. These consequences were the result of the fact that this individual faced a training load which was inappropriately high for his medical condition and hence a dispute arose whether the sports doctor, who has a duty to examine athletes, had properly

425. Article 1636 CL.
426. Torgāns, K.; Kārkliņš, J.; Bitāns, A. (2017), *supra* n. 70, 308.lpp.
427. *Ibid.*, 307.lpp.
428. Буковский, В. (1914), *supra* n. 150, c.1300.
429. Judgment of the Supreme Court of 17 Dec. 2019 in Case No. SKC-251/2019. Available at https://www.at.gov.lv/lv/tiesu-prakse/judikaturas-nolemumu-arhivs/civillietu-departaments/hronologiska-seciba?lawfilter=0&year=2019 [accessed on 25.11.2021]

assessed his health condition and properly notified the coach and the athlete's parents about those health conditions, and whether the coach had trained the athlete in line with the appropriate training plan and whether he had employed training methods inappropriate for athletes at the respective age. In particular, the dispute was about whether the coach used lead belts in order to impose extra resistance on the athlete. The Supreme Court, as cassation instance court, did not examine the case on its merits and thus did not assess whether the doctor and coach were at fault. However, the Supreme Court emphasized several elements which the appeal instance court had failed to examine properly and hence would have to examine again in order to establish whether there was contributory fault on the part of the doctor and coach. At the same time, those assessing this situation need to keep in mind that the sport of ice hockey, although hard and demanding and involving the risk of certain injuries, does not *per se* impose substantial risks for the health issues faced by the injured person in the given case. This means that, once the risks of particular injuries are not that high, the question of possible contributory fault comes into play.

*229.* This aspect was confirmed in an earlier case, which in its time attracted considerable publicity. In this case, the court examined a claim by relatives of deceased soldiers for compensation for non-pecuniary damage caused by the death of these soldiers during military parachute training, during which they fell into a river and drowned. As was later established on appeal, this situation was caused by negligence by the responsible officers.[430] In this situation, it should also be kept in mind that this tragic outcome appeared in the course of training, not a real military operation. In the latter case, the possible negligence of responsible officers perhaps would have had lesser significance as a real military action *per se* invokes a substantial risk of death.

*230.* This opinion is indirectly confirmed by another judgment in a case concerning injury suffered by a firefighter. The claimant, a former firefighter, had entered a partially collapsed shopping centre while performing his duties in order to rescue people injured by the collapse. At the time when he performed his duties, a second collapse occurred, causing him bodily injury. The injured former firefighter claimed pecuniary and non-pecuniary damage from the owners of the building and the company operating the shop. The court completely dismissed the claim, finding that the claimant had accepted the risk by undertaking the duties of a firefighter. In addition, the court analysed the social security provisions of firefighters, under which in case of injury or death the state provides compensation to the firefighter or their relatives. Therefore the court came to a conclusion that, under Latvia's legal system, the legislator had decided to regulate cases involving such injuries by means of special social security provisions rather than by general tort law. Moreover, the court emphasized that the collapse of the building was a catastrophe and in such cases everyone, including the owners of the building and operator of the shop located in the building, are required to obey the orders of firefighters and other emergency services. Therefore it was up to these services to decide how rescue

430. Judgment of the Supreme Court of 14 Jun. 2011 in Case No. PAC-0175. Not published.

operations were to be carried out. The owners of the building and operator of the shop cannot affect the course of these operations. Therefore they may not be held liable if someone is injured during the course of these operations.[431]

*231.* These findings of the court are correct and reasonable. In the given case, the injury is caused by the materialization of a risk which is directly related to the duties of firefighters to enter dangerous buildings and other dangerous places in order to rescue people. Entering these buildings and places may cause injury to the firefighters themselves, as this case shows. It should also be kept in mind that neither the owners of the building nor the operator of the shop had acted intentionally with the purpose of creating danger or inflicting damage. Otherwise, any such intentional actions could be considered as the direct cause of the damage (instead of materialization of professional risks), thus giving the right to claim compensation. Moreover, it should be kept in mind that if the owner of a building or operator of a shop is aware of their potential liability for injury to firefighters even without deliberate, intentional actions, this may prevent the owner and operator from timely calling the emergency services, which in turn might cause public danger. To avoid such consequences, damage should be compensated from the special social security funds designated by the legislator particularly for covering injury inflicted on firefighters and other employees of emergency services.

## §2. Necessity

*232.* Latvian law has no explicit provisions releasing from liability someone who causes damage to someone else when acting in an emergency. However, such a situation may be considered as self-help or self-defence, which are explicitly seen as valid justification in Latvian law. Both situations are discussed in the next subchapter.

## §3. Self-Help and Self-Defence

*233.* In order to be used as a justification, self-help and self-defence must be necessary and reasonable means of preventing damage to one's rights and legal interests.[432] These rights and legal interests are not limited to one's life or health, but cover protection of property and legal interests associated with property. However, self-help and self-defence arise from different branches of the law which may influence their scope of application.

*234.* On the one hand, self-defence is governed by property law. The possessor is allowed self-defence in order to defend possession[433] and the owner is entitled to

431. Judgment of Riga District Court of 27 Jul. 2016 in Case No. C33403316. Not published.
432. Article 1733 CL.
433. Article 913 CL.

self-defence in order to protect ownership.[434] The means of self-defence includes rights of detainer and distress which are remedies falling either within contract law (detainer rights) or tort law (distress).[435] These provisions may create the impression that rights to self-defence are rather broad, especially as the wording of the law even allows the owner to destroy the property of other persons if it is the sole means of protecting the owner's own property. However, in this context, the expression 'sole means' fully deserves emphasis, as court practice shows that self-defence does not justify violations of the rights and interests of others if other legally more correct or more reasonable methods are available.

*235.* The Supreme Court examined a case where the tenant of a dwelling house claimed damages from the owner. Before starting to live in the house, the tenant at their own cost had repaired the building. The lease contract explicitly allowed the repair, stating that the costs of repair would later be deducted from the lease payment. However, once the repair had been done and the tenant started to live in the house with their family, the owner started to object to the quality of repair and on this ground notified the tenant that the lease contract was terminated and the tenant must vacate the house and adjacent land plot. The tenant applied to the court for compensation by way of damages, which had not yet been deducted from the lease payments due to early termination of the lease contract. Note here that the owner terminated the lease agreement under special provisions in the lease agreement that was more favourable to the owner than those in the Law 'On Residental Tenancy' (*Par dzīvojamo telpu īri* in Latvian).[436] The law was adopted bearing in mind the specific situation in Latvia after the restoration of independence when the ownership of nationalized residential buildings was restored to former owners of these buildings and their heirs, causing various conflict situations between these owners and the tenants living in these houses. Therefore, in pursuit of social goals, the Latvian legislator adopted the Law 'On Residental Tenancy', which included provisions basically designed to protect tenants. The appeal instance court dismissed the tenant's claim, finding that the owner of the building had merely exercised their rights. However, the Supreme Court quashed the judgment of the appeal instance court, ruling that an owner may not exercise their rights in a manner contrary to the mandatory provisions of the Law.[437] Note: since 1 May 2021, this has been replaced by the new Dwelling Premises Rent Law.[438]

*236.* In another case, the claimant bought an advertising stand located on a land plot owned by another person as landlord. The landlord of the land plot notified the owner of the advertising stand that he must pay for the use of the land plot where

434. Article 1040 CL.
435. Article 1733 CL.
436. Law 'On Residential Tenancy'. Official translation into English available on the official web-page of the State Language Centre at https://vvc.gov.lv/image/catalog/dokumenti/On_Residential_Tenancy.doc [accessed on 15 Jan. 2022].
437. Judgment of the Supreme Court of 20 Jun. 2016 in Case No. SKC-244/2016. Available at https://www.at.gov.lv/lv/tiesu-prakse/judikaturas-nolemumu-arhivs/civillietu-departaments/hronologiska-seciba?lawfilter=0&year=2016 [accessed on 26 Nov. 2021].
438. Dwelling Premises Rent Law. No English translation is available.

the stand stood and invited the claimant to conclude a lease contract at short notice, failing which the advertising stand would be cut down and removed from the land. The board member of the owner of the advertising stand at that time was abroad and could not appear at the given time before the landlord in order to sign the lease contract. Hence the landlord, as threatened, cut down the advertising stand and removed it from the land, claiming to be protecting his property rights. The owner of the destroyed advertising stand claimed damages for the destroyed property. The appeal instance court dismissed the claim. However, the Supreme Court took a different view and ruled that a landlord who wants to remove an advertising stand from their land due to the absence of a lease contract or for any other reason should have applied to the court with a claim accordingly, but was not entitled deliberately to destroy someone else's property in order to protect their own if other means were available.[439]

*237.* Detainer rights means that a claimant in possession of a defendant's property is entitled to keep that property until their claim is satisfied.[440] The law specifies several situations in which someone is entitled to exercise detainer rights. As is emphasized in Latvian legal doctrine[441] and court practice,[442] detainer rights may be exercised only when explicitly allowed by law. Under the general provisions of the Civil Law, detainer rights belong (I) to the lessor of a fruit-bearing parcel of land in regard to production from the parcel of land and to the movable property of the lessee located there and the lessor may exercise those detainer rights in the case of late payment under the lease, as well as all other claims that might arise against a lessee on the basis of a lease; (II) to a lessor against a sub-lessee to whom the lessee has sub-leased their lessee rights; (III) to a person who rents out a building or premises therein, or an open lot not meant for fruit production. That person may exercise detainer rights regarding claims arising from the rental contract and apply to property of the tenant which the tenant has brought into the building or onto the lot for use or storage, including goods, but not intangible property and claims of the tenant, even if documents regarding such claims were brought there.[443] Additionally, special detainer rights are applicable in cases of commercial transactions. In particular, merchant A is entitled to retain the movable property and securities owned by merchant B (but in the hands of merchant A) which, in line with the will of merchant B, have come into the possession of merchant A by way of retainer on the basis of a commercial transaction, so that merchant A is entitled not to release any such property and securities as long as merchant A's money claim covered by

439. Judgment of the Supreme Court of 10 Mar. 2016 in Case No. SKC-70/2016. Available at https://www.at.gov.lv/lv/tiesu-prakse/judikaturas-nolemumu-arhivs/civillietu-departaments/hronologiska-seciba?lawfilter=0&year=2016 [accessed on 26 Nov. 2021].
440. Article 1734 CL.
441. Torgāns, K. (2018), *supra* n. 11, 179.lpp.
442. Judgment of the Supreme Court of 17 Oct. 2012 in Case No. SKC-579/2012. Available at https://www.at.gov.lv/lv/tiesu-prakse/judikaturas-nolemumu-arhivs/civillietu-departaments/hronologiska-seciba?lawfilter=0&year=2012 [accessed on 19 Jan. 2022].
443. Articles 1734–1736 CL.

the retainer arising from the commercial transaction entered into between merchant A and merchant B merchant is not satisfied.[444]

*238.* Distress rights are rights exercisable by the owner of a parcel of land or their substitute (user, lessee, manager, servants), (i) if someone else's domestic animal enters his land or (ii) if strangers intrude illegally thereon. By exercising distress rights, the owner or their substitute may catch and detain domestic animals, take property from persons, and (iii) personally detain a thief.[445]

## §4. Other

*239.* Important types of justification include an accidental event *(cas fortuit)* and force majeure (or *vis major).* These are in some sense unique, as they serve as justification for an alleged tortfeasor from two different perspectives.

*240.* First, as we have seen, the general form of civil liability in Latvia is fault-based liability, and fault may be represented via intention or negligence. An accidental event and force majeure are notions beyond the borders of fault. As Vladimir Bukovsky asserted, the existence of an accident excludes fault.[446] In other words, if the risk of accident materializes, it does not provide a ground for liability. Likewise, Čakste indicated that an accident may be further split between an accidental event and force majeure.[447] These are events that are objectively unforeseeable and unavoidable and hence completely beyond anyone's control.[448] An accidental event might in principle be avoided; however, it is unforeseeable, and therefore, it is subjectively unavoidable.[449] It may include various situations, for instance, illegal activity by third persons may be considered as an accidental event if others do not have reasonable grounds to foresee it.[450] Moreover, this foreseeability will be viewed from the perspective of the ordinary reasonable person (*paterfamilias* in Latin). If such a person could not foresee it, it may be considered as an accidental

444. Article 399 KCL.
445. Article 1741 CL.
446. Буковскій, В. (1914), *supra* n. 150, c.1391.
447. Čakste, K. Nejaušība un nepārvarama vara Latvijas Civillikumos *[Accident and force majeure in Latvian law].* Jurists, 1937, Nr. 71/72.
448. Van Dam, C. (2013), *supra* n. 332, p. 301.
449. Bērziņa, K. Nejaušs notikums un tā sekas *[Accidental Event and its Consequences].* Jurista Vārds, 2015, Nr.7, 29.lpp.
450. Kārkliņš, J. Nejaušs notikums, vainojamība un civiltiesiskā atbildība [*Cas Fortuit, Culpability and Civil Liability*]. Grām.: Jurisprudence un kultūra: pagātnes mācības un nākotnes izaicinājumi. Latvijas Universitātes 5.starptautiskā zinātniskā konference, veltīta Latvijas Universitātes Juridiskās fakultātes 95.gadadienai. 2014.gada 10–11.novembris, Rīga: Latvijas Universitāte, 2014, 508.lpp. Available in Latvian at *https://www.apgads.lu.lv/fileadmin/user_upload/lu_portal/apgads/PDF/Jur-konf-5_2014_Jur-Culture-Chall.pdf*; Обязательственное Право Губерній Прибалтійскихъ *[Law of Obligations of the Baltic Provinces].* (Изъ курса проф. Эрдмана). Переводъ и дополнительныя примѣчанія М. О. Гредингера. Изданіе почетнаго судьи Ф. Е. Камкина. 1908, стр. 205.

event, although an especially cautious and prudent person could have foreseen such a situation.[451]

*241.* At the beginning of the twentieth century, Bukovsky also opined that a situation where documents certifying the existence of certain rights or obligations were destroyed by fire should be treated as an accidental event because the manor house where these documents were kept fell victim to an attack by socialist revolutionaries.[452] Apart from the fact that it illustrates the sometimes gruesome reality of the twentieth century, this example very well illustrates that in case of an accidental event the criterion of foreseeability plays a major role in terms of the possibility to prevent damage caused. That is, if the owner of a manor house could foresee an attack by revolutionaries, he would probably store the documents elsewhere. Therefore, in this hypothetical example, the damage could have been prevented, but subjectively was not, as it could not reasonably have been foreseen.

*242.* A more contemporary example is a case examined by the Supreme Court in 2015. A passenger on public transport (bus) fell to the floor and was injured because the bus driver suddenly stopped the bus. However, the bus driver did so in order to avoid a potential accident which might be caused by a sudden or wrong manoeuvre by another driver. In such circumstances, the court found that the owner of the bus was not liable for the injuries to the passenger because from the perspective of the bus owner it was an accidental event.[453] Hence another important emphasis should here be added. That is, although a certain situation might be an accident from the perspective of one person (the bus owner in the case discussed), it might not be an accident from the perspective of someone else (for instance, the driver who made a wrong manoeuvre).

451. Čakste, K. (2011), *supra* n. 446.
452. Буковскій, B. (1914), *supra* n. 150, T. II, c.1392.
453. Judgment of the Supreme Court of 5 Mar. 2015 in Case No. SKC-250/2015. Not published.

## Chapter 3. Contributory Fault

*243.* Similarly to German law,[454] based on the principle of good faith, contributory fault by a victim who has suffered damage may completely or at least partially release the person who caused the damage from the obligation to compensate the victim. However, Latvian legal doctrine prefers to use the term 'mixed liability' or 'mixed fault' following the continental European tradition rather than the common-law term 'contributory fault' or 'contributory negligence'.[455]

*244.* Apart from general considerations in the context of the principle of good faith, Latvian law in general and Latvian tort law in particular stipulates other provisions in this respect. These provisions are different and depend on whether contributory fault appeared in the form of intent or negligence.

*245.* If both parties intentionally act with intent in respect to the same object, they cannot claim damages from one another. However, if only one party acts with intent, the other party may claim damages even though they acted negligently.[456] A situation where both parties acted with intent towards each other might be the context of a dispute between them on ownership over forest land and each party takes measures to decrease the value of the forest land so that if ownership is finally received by the opposite party, that party receives a less valuable property.[457] In such a case, neither party may claim damages from the other.

*246.* If both parties have committed negligence towards the other, their mutual claims for damage(s) are terminated by setoff to the extent they overlap.[458] Bukovsky asserted that if both parties acted negligently, they each may have claims for damage (unlike the situation analysed above, when both parties act with intent and where neither of them has a claim), but these claims are simply terminated by application of mutual setoff.[459]

*247.* Contributory fault is a justification of partial release from strict liability if it is to be applied. The Civil Law envisages that if the possessor of an object of abnormal danger loses possession over an object due to their own fault and someone else acquires it, then liability for damage is split between both persons according to the extent to which either of them is blameworthy for the damage.[460] This provision deserves attention in several aspects. First of all, although the respective provision stipulates strict liability irrespective of fault, either in the form of intent or negligence, it still requires evaluation as to whether the lawful possessor of an

454. Spindler & Rieckers, *supra* n. 397, p. 105.
455. Sinaiskis, V. (1996), *supra* n. 116, 149.lpp.
456. Article 1642 CL.
457. Torgāns, K. [Commentary of Article 1642 of the Civil Law], ram.: Latvijas Republikas Civillikuma komentāri. Saistību tiesības (1401–2400.p.) [*Commentary to the Civil Law of the Republic of Latvia. Law of Obligations (Arts 1401–2400)*]. (2000), 149.lpp.
458. Article 1650 CL.
459. Буковскiй, В. (1914), *supra* n. 150, c.1308.
460. Article 2347(2) CL.

object of abnormal danger loses possession due to their own fault. If they lost possession without fault, for example, in the result of a robbery, which should be seen as an accidental event, i.e., the lawful possessor does not have reason to foresee a robbery and the robbery was executed in a manner that avoided all means of the possessor's reasonable precaution, then the possessor will be completely released from liability. However, a possessor who acted negligently at least – for instance, by failing to take all reasonable precautionary measures in order to prevent robbery – will be partially liable for the damage caused. The co-authors of this monograph have not come across any notable example where this provision was applied by the court. However, a hypothetical example could be when someone who, on legally valid grounds, stores dangerous chemicals or explosives but forgets to switch on the alarm system in the building where these substances are stored and subsequently someone steals these substances from storage and later these substances cause damage to a third party.

*248.* Opinions in Latvian legal doctrine differ as to how to treat this situation. Latvian legal scholar and practitioner Agris Bitāns indicates that in such a case, liability for damage caused will be split between the lawful possessor of the object of great danger and the person who stole it.[461] Torgāns is of a different opinion, emphasizing that reference to fault in this context is somewhat misleading and that in other countries in similar cases the law requires split liability between the lawful and illegal possessors according to the contribution of each of them to the accident which caused the damage.[462] This latter opinion could prevail as it provides a fairer resolution of the situation in cases where, although the lawful possessor acted negligently, they far less substantially contributed to the situation where a third party sustained damage. An illustration of this situation could be that the illegal possessor has further elaborated on the dangerous substances or acted with them in such a way as to substantially increase the risk of damage.

461. Bitāns, A. [Commentary of Article 2347 of the Civil Law], ram.: Latvijas Republikas Civillikuma komentāri. Saistību tiesības (1401–2400.p.) [*Commentary to the Civil Law of the Republic of Latvia. Law of Obligations (Arts 1401–2400)*]. (2000), 629.lpp.
462. Torgāns, K. (2018), *supra* n. 11, 481.lpp.

## Chapter 4. Exemption Clauses

*249.* Following the principle of freedom of contract, contractual parties are free to agree on various exemptions of liability and also on limitation of the amount of damages to be compensated, given that such agreement is concluded without defects of consent such as mistake, fraud or duress. The right to derogate from entitlement to compensatory damages or modify the substance or amount of damages to be compensated applies to the damage caused by breach of an agreement, as well as to damage caused by tort. The parties may also agree that compensation of damages caused by breach of agreement is limited either by amount or by type, provided that only a certain type (usually only direct damage) should be compensated.[463]

*250.* However, the Civil Law expressly stipulates separate mandatory provisions from which the parties may not derogate by means of agreement such as an agreement in advance not to compensate damage from an act committed with wrongful intent, unless such derogation refers to damage already inflicted.[464] The idea of this provision is that the injured person is aware of certain damage and the fact that a certain person intentionally caused it but, nevertheless, the injured person is willing to give up their claim. It is unclear from the Civil Law what other mandatory provisions on the compensation of damage cannot be derogated from.

*251.* A similar idea applies to the possibility of releasing members of a company board or council from liability to compensate for damage caused to the company. A meeting of shareholders may release the members of these institutions from liability in damages caused to the company.[465] However, as is provided in settled court practice, such relief may only be attributed to damages which are known to the shareholders at the moment when their decision to release is adopted.[466] At the same time, a board or council member who proves that they acted in good faith and in line with the decision of the meeting of shareholders (for instance, to conclude a particular transaction, commence production of a new product or enter a new market) may exculpate themself from liability.[467]

463. Article 1785 CL.
464. Article 1643 CL.
465. Article 173(1) KCL.
466. Judgment of the Supreme Court of 24 Apr. 2019 in Case No. SKC-46/2019. Available at https://www.at.gov.lv/lv/tiesu-prakse/judikaturas-nolemumu-arhivs/civillietu-departaments/hronologiska-seciba?lawfilter=0&year=2019 [accessed on 29 Nov. 2021]
467. Article 169(4) KCL.

# Part V. Causation

## Chapter 1. Introduction

*252.* Similarly, as in the case of other countries, Latvian law (as well as Latvian court practice and Latvian legal literature) is familiar with the concept of causation in general and the causal link in particular. Though the concept of causation is shared by all types of legal liability envisaged by Latvian law,[468] yet the understanding of it may be different depending on the type of legal liability, each of which is subject to different regulation.[469]

*253.* Causation in Latvian civil law is perceived in the objective sense.[470] This means that the court must assess the existence of a causal link from the objective standpoint by establishing whether particular illegal conduct either in the form of an act or omission (lack of activity) as a cause may lead to the amount of damage because of that conduct. So mere subjective understanding by either the victim or the tortfeasor as to a particular causal relationship should not be taken into account.

*254.* As discussed *infra* in the next chapter of this part of the monograph, Latvian civil law contains few direct or indirect references to the need to establish a causal link. Likewise, current Latvian court practice is not fully clear concerning the use of a particular causation theory, despite the fact that these theories are widely discussed in Latvian legal literature under strong influence of the adequacy theory.[471] However, as rightly noted in European tort law literature, the understanding of causation and its implications is grounded on policy considerations specific to each particular jurisdiction.[472] Latvia is no exception in this situation, so this part of the monograph will be devoted to discussion of the Latvian national approach to causation, especially from the perspective of Latvian tort law.

*255.* Causation is involved in Latvian civil law from the standpoint of several situations. Each of these is discussed in detail in its own separate sub-chapter.

468. I.e., civil liability, criminal liability, administrative liability, and disciplinary liability.
469. Mantrovs, V. Cēloniskā sakara izpratnes jautājumi civiltiesību kontekstā [*Issues of the Understanding of Causation in the Context of Civil Law*]. Jurista vārds, 2016, Nr.13.
470. Torgāns, K. Līgumu un deliktu tiesību problēmas. Rīga: Tiesu namu aģentūra, 2013, 194.lpp.; Mantrovs, V. (2016 a), *supra* n. 469.
471. *See* next sub-chapter of this monograph.
472. Van Dam, C. (2013), *supra* n. 332, pp. 307–308.

## Chapter 2. Causal Link as a Civil Liability Precondition

*256.* One of the most common and important implications of causation in Latvian tort law relates to the situation when a causal link is perceived as a civil liability precondition.[473] Similarly to other European countries, Latvian civil law does not explicitly regulate causation as a civil liability precondition. However, a causal link as a civil liability precondition may be deduced from the whole body of Latvian civil (and also tort) law as well as separate norms of Latvian civil law.

*257.* Article 1635(1) of the Civil Law is considered to be the basic norm for establishing civil liability in Latvia. This basic civil liability norm indirectly requires the existence of a causal link as a civil liability precondition. This provision envisages, *inter alia*, that every legal infringement (*tiesību aizskārums* in Latvian)[474] resulting in harm must be compensated. As one may observe from the phrase 'resulting in', this expression demonstrates the necessity for a causal link in establishing civil liability in every situation when it is invoked. Therefore, a causal link as a precondition for civil liability could already be deduced from the basic norm for establishing civil liability.

*258.* It has to be said that there are a few self-contradictory Latvian court judgments stating that a causal link need not be established as a precondition for civil liability. For instance, in one case, the Supreme Court (wrongly in the opinion of the co-authors of this monograph) admitted that a causal link need not be established in the case of an assignor's liability over an assigned contract object:

> The Supreme Court agrees with the person who submitted the cassation appeal that a causal link does not fall within the list of the preconditions that had to be established in order to find the basis for the alienator's liability for damages caused by the defects of the alienated thing. [..] the alienator shall be liable for damages if it is established 1) a hidden defect; 2) time of occurrence of defects (before alienation); 3) their significance (*see* Article 1613 of the Civil Law); 4) the wrongful intent of the alienator, which manifests itself in one or more of the ways defined in Article 1620 of the Civil Law in the failure to disclose or concealment of defects, or in a declaration that the thing has certain characteristics. In view of the above, the Supreme Court acknowledges that the [appeal instance] court had no legal basis to extend the above-mentioned criteria by also including assessment of a causal link, as it consequently applied

---

473. Illegal conduct, amount of damage, and fault are other preconditions for civil liability. For discussion, *see* Pt. I of this monograph *supra*.

474. The official translation of the Civil Law uses the term 'tort' instead. However, use of this term is not precise. The basic civil liability norm is of more general application by covering not only torts but also infringements of obligations established on other grounds (i.e., contract or *ex lege*).

> simultaneously both general and special regulation for assessment of compensation of damages, which in the present case could lead to ungrounded release of the alienator from liability concerning the shortcomings of the alienated thing.[475]

As one may observe from this quote from a Supreme Court judgment, the court's conclusion that there is 'no legal basis to extend the above-mentioned criteria by also including assessment of a causal link' contradicts the court's own finding concerning the fourth criterion, which actually presupposes a causal link. Therefore, the conclusion of the Supreme Court in this case is self-contradictory and the logic of excluding a causal link from evaluation in the given case is open to doubt.

*259.* Likewise, a similar rule concerning a causal link as a precondition for liability is available in the case of claiming damages as a universal remedy under Latvian civil law.[476] Indeed, under Article 1779 of the Civil Law (the basic norm for the duty to compensate damages), everyone has a duty to compensate for losses they have caused through their acts or failure to act. The expression 'caused through' undoubtedly, though indirectly, refers to the existence of a causal link as a precondition for the duty to compensate damages. It is clear from this discussion why this Article serves to substantiate the existence of such a precondition. At the same time, a causal link as a precondition for compensation of damages may also be deduced from Article 1775 of the Civil Law envisaging that compensation will be payable for any loss which is not accidental.[477]

*260.* In some provisions regulating certain torts, a causal link is explicitly mentioned as a precondition either for civil liability in general or damages in particular. A good illustration of such a situation is product liability. Article 11(2) of the Law *On Liability for Defects of Goods and Services* envisages that:

> [t]he injured person has a duty to prove the loss, the defect of goods or services and the causal relationship [causal link – authors' remark] between the defect of goods or services and losses.

This provision seems to be unique in Latvian civil law as it contains all liability preconditions for claiming damages. These are listed *numerus clausus,* including a causal link. Another implication of this provision relates to envisaging the *onus probandi* on the part of the victim to prove all these preconditions.

475. Judgment of the Supreme Court of 30 Jun. 2017 in Case No SKC-216/2017 (C31357712), Point 9.2. Available in Latvian at https://at.gov.lv/downloadlawfile/5176.
476. Torgāns, K. (2018), *supra* n. 11, 199.lpp.
477. Torgāns, K. [Commentary of Article 1775 of the Civil Law], onf.: Latvijas Republikas Civillikuma komentāri. Saistību tiesības (1401–2400.p.) [Commentary to the Civil Law of the Republic of Latvia. Law of Obligations (Arts 1401–2400)]. (2000), 270.lpp.

*261.* As is clear from Articles 1635(1) and 1779 of the Civil Law discussed *supra*, the Civil Law is familiar with the *conditio sine qua non* theory (test). Application of this rule is directly admitted in Latvian civil law literature by analyzing its application in Latvian civil law.[478]

*262.* However, it is more difficult to state which theory is used by Latvian courts in the situation when the *conditio sine qua non* theory (test) cannot be employed, particularly if damage results from several causes. At the same time, Latvian civil law scholars constantly point to the application of the *adequacy theory* (test) but so far no opinion has doubted the application of this theory in Latvian civil law.[479] Application of the adequacy test was already recognized in Latvian civil law literature of the 1930s. Indeed, Čakste noted that the adequacy theory is the leading theory in Latvian court practice and literature.[480] Moreover, the adequacy theory is the most suitable for Latvian civil law as may be deduced from the overall structure of regulation of civil-law relationships in Latvia.

*263.* It seems that Latvian court practice is based on the adequacy theory as well, although this has so far not been explicitly mentioned in any Latvian court judgment.[481]

*264.* A good illustration of this unclear situation is the following case reviewed at all three Latvian court instances and later discussed in Latvian civil-law literature. During an operation, a surgical instrument – a Reverdin spatula (25x10 cm in size) – was left in the patient's abdominal cavity, which caused permanent pain there for several years after the operation. This instrument was later discovered and removed during a subsequent operation. A dispute arose over whether the negative consequences in the form of pain and distress were the cause of the pain all the time until the second operation or just for a while after the first operation. The appeal instance court established that the cause of the pain could have been established during the stay in a medical institution during the initial operation. However, the Supreme Court disagreed and reached the following conclusion:

> There is no doubt that the consequences of the conduct of the defendant's medical personnel were the cause of the pain in the claimant's mid-abdomen both immediately after the operation and thereafter.[482]

---

478. Mantrovs, V. Cēloniskā sakara problēmjautājumi civiltiesību kontekstā [*Problem Issues of Causal Link in the Context of Civil Law*]. Jurista vārds, 2016, Nr.16.
479. Kārkliņš, J. Nejaušs notikums, vainojamība un civiltiesiskā atbildība [Cas Fortuit, Culpability and Civil Liability]. Grām.: Jurisprudence un kultūra: pagātnes mācības un nākotnes izaicinājumi. Latvijas Universitātes 5.starptautiskā zinātniskā konference, veltīta Latvijas Universitātes Juridiskās fakultātes 95.gadadienai. 2014.gada 10.–11.novembris, Rīga: Latvijas Universitāte, 2014, 503.lpp. Available in Latvian at *https://www.apgads.lu.lv/fileadmin/user_upload/lu_portal/apgads/PDF/Jur-konf-5_2014_Jur-Culture-Chall.pdf*; Torgāns, K., Kārkliņš, J. (2015), *supra* n. 117; Kārkliņš, J. (2015), *supra* n. 131, 164.lpp.; Mantrovs, V. (2016 b), *supra* n. 478.
480. Čakste, K. (2011), *supra* n. 69, 99.lpp.
481. Mantrovs, V. (2016 b), *supra* n. 478.
482. Judgment of the Supreme Court of 28 Jan. 2015 in Case No SKC-9/2015 (C30576709).

As is clear from this quote, the Latvian court reasoning in this judgment actually led to application of the adequacy theory as argued in Latvian civil-law literature.[483] However, this theory was not explicitly mentioned by the Supreme Court in its judgment.

483. *See* Mantrovs, V. (2016 b), *supra* n. 478.

## Chapter 3. Causal Link and Its Influence on Classification of Damages

*265.* Another necessity for causation to be taken into account relates to the duty to compensate damages. One of the *classifications of damages* recognized in Latvian civil-law literature relates to dividing damages into *direct, indirect, and incidental* damages. This classification is based on the regulation of the Civil Law itself. Indeed, Article 1773 of the Civil Law states that:

> [a] loss shall be considered: direct where it is the natural and inevitable result of an illegal act or failure to act; indirect where it is caused by an occurrence of particular circumstances or relationships; and accidental where caused by a chance event or *force majeure*.

As is clear from this quoted provision, classification of damages as envisaged in this Article is based on the relationship between an illegal activity and damage it causes, i.e., the causal link between the illegal activity as the cause and the damage as its consequence. However, it should be noted that this classification concerns types of damages but not types of causal link, i.e. this classification of damages depends on the relationship of damages with illegal activity as a cause.[484] These reasons clearly explain that the rule according to which no one should compensate for incidental damages arises from the consideration that it is not possible to establish a causal link between such damages and the particular illegal activity.[485]

*266.* As is rightly indicated in legal literature, the classification of damages has a secondary meaning as it helps to differentiate cases when damage (i.e. harm) should not be compensated, i.e., in the case of accidental damages.[486] However, this conclusion relates to general regulation for compensation of damages and does not mean that incidental damages should not be compensated at all. Incidental damages may be compensated by an insurer, in certain cases prescribed by law, for instance, default, or if a contractual party agrees to assume liability for a risk.[487] Likewise, classification of damages into direct and indirect may have a practical meaning.[488]

*267.* Another issue in regulation of damages when a causal link should be taken into account is *remoteness of damage*. Remoteness of damage is explicitly covered in Article 1779.[1] of the Civil Law which was introduced as recently as 2009. This provision states that:

> [a] person who causes losses shall compensate losses in an amount which could have been reasonably foreseen upon entering into a transaction as

484. Torgāns K. (2013), *supra* n. 456, 197-.198.lpp.
485. *Ibid.*
486. Torgāns, K. (2018), *supra* n. 11, 226.lpp.
487. *Ibid.*, 207.lpp.
488. For a discussion of direct and indirect damages in Latvia and consequences of such division, *see* Ch. 2 of Pt. VI of this monograph *infra*.

> expected consequences of non-performance, unless such non-performance occurred through malicious intention or [gross] negligence.

In the case of remoteness of damage, the causal link manifests in the consideration of whether a person could reasonably have foreseen damage or not. As is indicated in Latvian legal literature, remoteness of damage is closely connected with the existence of a causal link as different unfavourable events, such as natural catastrophes, could not be considered a direct cause since they are too remote.[489]

489. Torgāns, K. (2018), *supra* n. 11, 232.lpp.

# Chapter 4. Causal Link as a Precondition for Establishing Certain Illegal Activities

*268.* Causal link is also considered as one of the preconditions for certain illegal conduct such as fraud and duress, both being types of defect of will. Though these situations fall outside the topic of this monograph, they will be discussed for the sake of completeness.

*269. Fraud* is considered a defect of will when one person induces another person to conclude a legal transaction in a non-violent but illegal way.[490] Fraud is explicitly regulated in[491] Article 1459 of the Civil Law, which contains the legal definition of the term 'fraud' by envisaging that:

> [f]raud is the illegal deception of another person for the purpose of inducing him or her to perform acts in contravention to his or her interests or to refrain from such acts.
> By interpreting this provision, Balodis indicates that a causal link must be established between deception and the expression of will of the party induced to enter into a transaction by fraud.[492] So in this case a causal link is included in the elements of fraud as one of its preconditions.

*270.* Similarly, a causal link must also be established in the case of *duress*. Duress means that a person is forced to express an expression of intent which is contrary to their interests.[493] Duress is also explicitly regulated in the Civil Law.[494] Article 1463 of the Civil Law clarifies the term 'duress' by stating that:

> [d]uress may consist of physical force or of threats which induce fear in a person. When physical force is used, there is no expression of intent and there is no act by the person under duress.

In commenting on preconditions for duress, Balodis, among others, rightly refers to the need to establish a causal link between threat and involvement of the victim in a legal transaction.[495] The nature of manifestation of a causal link in this case viewed as a threat is a cause for fear on the part of the victim, so that fear is a reason for this person to express the will necessary to conclude the legal transaction.[496] Thus it is not possible to establish the existence of duress and, therefore, dispute the validity of a legal transaction if a causal link is not established between the fact of threat and fear caused, on the one hand, and the expression of will determined by exposure to the threat, on the other.

---

490. Balodis, K. (2007), *supra* n. 69, 266.lpp.
491. Articles 1459–1462 CL.
492. Balodis, K. (2007), *supra* n. 69, 269.lpp.
493. *Ibid.*, 272.lpp.
494. Articles 1463–1468 CL.
495. Balodis, K. (2007), *supra* n. 69, 274.lpp.
496. *Ibid.*, 275.lpp.

# Part VI. Remedies

## Chapter 1. General Principles

*271.* Every violation of a right affects the victim's financial or health condition. The legal system must ensure that a person whose property or health interests have been harmed is entitled to claim compensation or satisfaction. The various legal instruments that the victim may use against the tortfeasor are referred to as remedies.[497] These instruments are set by the Civil Law and other legal acts, but are scattered in different sections of these legal acts and are not codified under a single heading. For this reason, remedies should not be regarded as a unified legal institute but as a doctrinal category.[498]

*272.* Compensation is the main remedy in the case of damages. The goal of compensation is to ensure the fullest possible restoration of the situation that would have been if the tort had not occurred. This understanding of the purpose of compensation of damages is also recognized by the Supreme Court.[499] At the same time, it is not always possible to fully and accurately re-establish damaged property or a previous condition. For example, a unique painting cannot be replaced and injuries from a car accident cannot always be cured completely. It is, therefore, necessary to speak of pecuniary compensation or other financial value and recovery of the amount of property in the previous state 'as far as possible'.[500]

*273.* Settled court practice includes a more detailed and content-specific explanation of the purpose of compensation of damages. In this regard, the Supreme Court drew the following conclusion:

> Damages are of a financial nature, and the specific amount of compensation is established by resolving the dispute. The purpose of compensation of damages, in particular, is to restore to the fullest extent possible the situation of the victim's property that would have existed if the wrongful act had not occurred. In other words, the fundamental task of full compensation of damages is to prevent (at least minimize or mitigate) the negative effects of damage (i.e. harm)

497. Torgāns, K. (2018), *supra* n. 11, 173.lpp.
498. *Ibid.*, 175.lpp.
499. Judgment of the Supreme Court of 28 Jun. 2017 in Case No. SKC-215/2017 (C27148913), point 7.1.1.
500. Torgāns, K. (2018), *supra* n. 11, 199.lpp.

caused to property. Damage caused to property could result in reduction in the value of the property, additional expenses, lost profits and could be compensated either by restoring the former state of the property or by compensating reduction of the property's value.[501]

501. Judgment of the Supreme Court of 7 Jun. 2016 in Case No. SKC-7/2016 (C39072411), point 9.

# Chapter 2. Kinds of Damages

## §1. Individual and Collective Damages

*274.* In the case of damage (i.e., harm), the person who owned the property at the time of the damage caused or who had it in their possession, or the person who incurred expenses because of a wrongful act, such as medical costs, is entitled to compensation for damages (i.e., losses).[502] It is much more difficult to identify subjects who are entitled to compensation in cases of non-pecuniary damage such as long-term health dysfunction or death of a family member. The Civil Law does not identify an exact group of people who are entitled to compensation in these situations.[503] This is because the Civil Law was drafted in the 1930s (it entered into force on 1 January 1938) but non-pecuniary damage was recognized in Latvia and other European countries only in recent years.[504]

*275.* In cases of long-term injury or death of family members, damage should be compensated to the family as one victim and not to each family member individually.[505] However, there is no common understanding of the concept of family in Latvia. Even if there were such an understanding, it could not eliminate all uncertainties in the application of civil liability for compensation of non-pecuniary damage. A problem arises particularly in cases where the relationship between family members is poor or even hostile, i.e., when the claimants themselves do not regard themselves as a single family. Each member of the family may bring individual claims in different courts and even the requirements and basis and subject matters may vary.[506]

## §2. Direct and Indirect Damages

*276.* 264. As already stated in Part V of this monograph, Article 1773 of the Civil Law classifies damages in three kinds based on the relation with the cause of an occurrence:

> A loss shall be considered: direct where it is the natural and inevitable result of an illegal act or failure to act; indirect where it is caused by an occurrence of particular circumstances or relationships; and accidental when caused by a fortuitous event or force majeure.

502. Torgāns, K.; Kārkliņš, J.; Bitāns, A. (2017), *supra* n. 70, 273–274.lpp.
503. *Ibid.*, 274–275.lpp.
504. Lībiņa-Egnere, I. Personības tiesību aizsardzība un civiltiesiskā atbildība to aizskāruma gadījumā. Promocijas darbs [*Protection of Individual Rights and Civil Liability in Case of Violation Doctoral Thesis*]. Latvijas Universitāte, Rīga: 2006, 142.lpp.
505. Torgāns, K.; Kārkliņš, J.; Bitāns, A. (2017), *supra* n. 70, 276–277.lpp. With reference to: Judgment of the Supreme Court of 9 Feb. 2011 in Case No. SKC-56/2011, point 12.
506. Torgāns, K.; Kārkliņš, J.; Bitāns, A. (2017), *supra* n. 70, 278.lpp.

The breakdown of damages by their connection with the wrongful act is of secondary importance since Article 1773 formally only helps to distinguish between cases where damage should or should not be compensated (accidental damages).[507]

*277.* Under the general principle in Article 1775 of the Civil Law, any non-accidental damages must be compensated (both direct and indirect damages).[508] The term 'indirect damages' refers to damages related to a tort resulting from special circumstances but not being a necessary consequence. In such cases, the impairment along with other circumstances caused negative consequences.[509] This should be taken into consideration when evaluating causation.[510]

*278.* As discussed in previous chapters, causation in the Civil Law is understood as a legal connection between a person's wrongful act and damage that occurred.[511] The Civil Law sets several different standards of proof for causation. There is a difference between the standard of proof for direct and indirect damages. In legal doctrine, it has been stated that the standard of proof for indirect damages should be equal to the standard of proof for lost profits – proven to a level that would be credible as legal evidence that such detriment resulted.[512] As stated in court practice, indirect damages from the perspective of causation occurs due to several simultaneous or consecutive causes and could be caused not only by the tortfeasor's wrongful act.[513]

## §3. Pecuniary and Non-pecuniary Damage

*279.* Damages results in a reduction of wealth. In this regard, Article 1770 of the Civil Law states:

> A loss shall be understood to mean any deprivation which can be assessed financially.
> Compensation of damages has the function of compensating a reduction in the victim's wealth. Damages within the meaning of Article 1770 of the Civil Law are to be considered as any reduction, loss of, or damage to property, as well

507. With reference to: Judgment of the Supreme Court of 12 Jan. 2017 in Case No. SKC-5/2017 (C37105312), point 6.
508. Judgment of the Supreme Court of Latvia of 22 Nov. 2013 in Case No. SKC-318/2013 (C30445909), point 7.1.
509. Torgāns, K.; Kārkliņš, J.; Bitāns, A. (2017), *supra* n. 70, 171.lpp.
510. For a detailed discussion of causation in Latvia, *see* Pt. V of this monograph *supra*.
511. Mantrovs, V. (2016 a), *supra* n. 469.
512. Буковскій, В. (1914), *supra* n. 150, c.1390.
513. Judgment of the Supreme Court of 22 Nov. 2013 in Case No. SKC-318/2013 (C30445909), point 7.1.

as the consequences of an infringement of other rights of a pecuniary character.[514] As noted in legal doctrine, by damages the law understands damage to property or the difference that occurs before and after a wrongful act.[515]

*280.* The funds necessary to restore the previous state of a victim's wealth is the criterion for determining the extent to which the victim's pecuniary interests have suffered. Therefore, the fact that the victim themself has restored their wealth plays no decisive role and does not provide a basis for exemption of the tortfeasor's civil liability. In the light of this conclusion, a reduction of the victim's wealth that can be measured in money will be considered to be a 'deprivation which can be assessed financially' (*mantiski novērtējams pametums* in Latvian) within the meaning of Article 1770 of the Civil Law.[516]

*281.* In Latvian tort law, after the establishment of a wrongful act and causation between the tort and the damages caused, the tortfeasor is liable to compensate even if the amount of damages was unpredictable. This is because, in contrast to contract law, a wrongful act in tort law is unpredictable and the victim cannot prepare for it or use legal instruments to avoid it. However, under both contract law and tort law, a victim has an obligation to mitigate damages to the point that is reasonable.[517] This principle is set both in Article 1776[518] and Article 1 of the Civil Law.

*282.* Non-pecuniary damage is an impairment to a person or their legally protected interests that do not result in the reduction of wealth. Although no one has the right to impair the legally protected interests of others, not every harmful act needs to be compensated. First of all, non-pecuniary damage must be legally significant. Not all impairments of a person's mental well-being will be considered legally significant.[519]

*283.* Although Article 1635 of the Civil Law does not refer to significance as a necessary criterion, it is established in Latvian court practice that minor non-pecuniary damage should not be compensated. This is based on an indication in Article 1635(2) of the Civil Law that the amount of compensation for non-pecuniary damage should be determined by a court at its own discretion, taking into

514. Judgment of the Supreme Court of 6 Dec. 2013 in Case No. SKC-432/2013 (C04127299), point 11.
515. Torgāns, K.; Kārkliņš, J.; Bitāns, A. (2017), *supra* n. 70, 270–271.lpp.
516. Judgment of the Supreme Court of Latvia of 7 Jun. 2016 in Case No. SKC-7/2016 (C39072411), point 11.2.2.
517. Torgāns, K.; Kārkliņš, J.; Bitāns, A. (2017), *supra* n. 70, 271.lpp.
518. Article 1776 of the Civil Law states: 'A victim shall take such measures for prevention of losses which are reasonable under the relevant circumstances. A tortfeasor may request reduction of damages in such amount in which a victim could have through the exercise of due care (Art. 1646) prevented the loss except in a case of malicious infringement of rights. A victim has the right to claim compensation for such losses from which he could not avoid by taking the measures referred to this Article.'
519. Torgāns, K.; Kārkliņš, J.; Bitāns, A. (2017), *supra* n. 70, 272.lpp.

account the seriousness and the consequences of the non-pecuniary damage. Consequently, the seriousness and consequences of non-pecuniary damage may be considered to be minor and non-reimbursable. The division of non-pecuniary damage into 'reimbursable non-pecuniary damage' and 'non-reimbursable non-pecuniary damage' is also acknowledged in court practice.[520]

*284.* Second, it is important whether the damage caused is not too remote. Not all mental suffering establishes a subjective right to claim compensation for damage. If someone on the street sees a fatal car crash then, although such a sight is unpleasant, it does not give the right to bring an action in court. Therefore, the fact that some events have a negative impact on a person's mental health does not mean that all such harm should be compensated. Non-pecuniary damage should be compensated if the tortfeasor has significantly impaired the victim's legally protected non-pecuniary interests.[521]

*285.* The words 'compensation' and 'award of compensation' used in laws and court judgments are misleading, as they may and have created a misconception that the court must measure the extent of non-pecuniary damage, even though pain and suffering cannot be measured in money. The purpose of 'compensation' for non-pecuniary damage is not to compensate but to determine, on the basis of other criteria, what would reasonably be necessary to comfort the victim. In practice, claimants and courts in non-pecuniary damage cases sometimes mistakenly seek the same criteria for measuring compensation as for damages, i.e., compensation of pecuniary damage, where the loss has to be measured in monetary equivalents.[522]

## §4. Pure Economic Damages

*286.* Traditionally, damages resulting from impairment of rights has been contrasted with so-called pure economic damages (pure economic loss). For example, after a car crash, those who suffer are not only those whose cars have been damaged but also those who are forced to wait as a result of congestion and, for example, miss a flight. However, under Latvian tort law, people forced to wait because of congestion cannot claim compensation. If everyone suffering from minor daily incidents could claim compensation for all economic damages, the extent of liability would be unlimited. However, in some situations, pure economic damages should be compensated. A clear example could be the following situation: 'The applicant is unlawfully excluded from a professional organization, which leads to

---

520. Latvijas Republikas Augstākā tiesa. Tiesu prakses apkopojums 'Morālā kaitējuma atlīdzināšana civillietās' [*Supreme Court of the Republic of Latvia. Summary of Court Practice 'Compensation for Non-Pecuniary Damage in Civil Matters'*]. 2014, 29.lpp. Available in Latvian at https://at.gov.lv/lv/tiesu-prakse/tiesu-prakses-apkopojumi/civiltiesibas [accessed 29 Jul. 2021].
521. Torgāns, K.; Kārkliņš, J.; Bitāns, A. (2017), *supra* n. 70, 273.lpp.
522. Latvijas Republikas Augstākā tiesa. Tiesu prakses apkopojums 'Morālā kaitējuma atlīdzināšana civillietās' [*Supreme Court of the Republic of Latvia. Summary of Court Practice 'Compensation for Non-Pecuniary Damage in Civil Matters'*]. 2014, 9.lpp. Available: https://at.gov.lv/lv/tiesu-prakse/tiesu-prakses-apkopojumi/civiltiesibas [accessed 29 Jul. 2021].

unemployment and, consequently, lost profits. Although membership of this organization is not an absolute right, it can still be considered a legally protected interest and cannot be harmed.'[523]

*287.* Compensation for pure economic damages in the Latvian legal system should be looked at through the understanding of damages. The legal definition of the term 'damages' is given in Article 1770 of the Civil Law. This legal definition does not contain any restrictions on the origin of the damages.[524] But Article 1635 of the Civil Law declares when damage is to be compensated. It can be concluded from the legal definitions in Articles 1770 and 1635 of the Civil Law that a tortfeasor must compensate for all damages caused by a wrongful non-contractual act (tort). This is also confirmed by Article 1784 of the Civil Law: 'If a person suffers losses from the illegal actions of another person outside the scope of contractual relations, the person causing the losses shall be liable for all such losses.' As this definition suggests, neither Latvian Civil Law nor Latvian tort law specifically regulates compensation for pure economic damages. The Latvian legal system does not give rights to victims to compensation for pure economic damages. Even a tortfeasor's degree of fault or criminal liability cannot be used as a ground for compensation of pure economic damages.

## §5. Actual and Future Damages: Lost Profits

*288.* Article 1771 of the Civil Law for compensation of damages states:

> Losses [i.e. damages in the terminology of this monograph – authors' remark] may be either such losses as have already arisen or such losses as are anticipated; in the former case they give rise to a right to compensation, but in the latter case to a right to security.

Article 1771 of the Civil Law indicates a distinction between situations when the victim is entitled to compensation by way of damages or security. It sets a precondition for compensation of damages – the damages should actually exist at that time of the claim. If damages are only anticipated, there are no grounds for a claim for compensation. When a victim has suffered damages that still persists, this gives them the right to security.[525] In that light, a further explanation of anticipated damages is first required.

*289.* The Civil Law does not clearly define anticipated damages. In court practice, it has been noted that the function of anticipated damages is to prevent damage that may occur in the future but not to deal with the damage that already exists.[526]

523. Strazdiņš, Ģ. Civillikuma 1635. panta atbildības priekšnoteikumi [*Preconditions for Liability of Article 1635 of the Civil Law*]. Jurista Vārds, 2018, Nr.44.
524. Torgāns, K.; Kārkliņš, J.; Bitāns, A. (2017), *supra* n. 70, 206–207.lpp.
525. Judgment of the Supreme Court of 7 Jun. 2016 in Case No. SKC-7/2016 (C39072411), point 9.
526. *Ibid.*, point 11.2.

Anticipated damages cannot be clearly identified before a wrongful act. The possible amount may be discussed by the parties and assessed with a view to establishing a reasonable security. Security might take the form of a pledge or a mortgage, for instance. Provision for damages may also by its economic nature be subject to contractual penalties, although on the legal side it has the function of supplementing the burden of damages.[527]

*290.* In the analysis of the damages already arisen an important aspect is that it consists of two components. These are specified in Article 1772 of the Civil Law:

> A loss which has already arisen may be a diminution of the victim's present property or a decrease in his or her anticipated profits.

This division is taken from Roman Law.[528] First to explain is the reduction of current property.

*291.* According to the purpose of monetary compensation, reduction of current property means not only a decrease in the victim's property but also an increase in the victim's liabilities or property liabilities as a result of a tort. This conclusion accepts the notion in Latvian legal literature that an increase in the victim's property liabilities is equivalent to a 'loss of property' or a 'reduction in current property'. This is consistent with German and Swiss law.[529] In some cases, the existence of a right may be interpreted as a property of the person so that violation of this right should be considered as a reduction of current property.[530]

*292.* Second to explain is a loss of victim's expected profit. Lost profits are all those goods that were not yet on the victim's property at the time of the unlawful act that caused the damage but would have ended up there if that act had not been committed. Consequently, the purpose of compensating for lost profits is not to restore the previous situation but to put the victim in the material position they would have been in if the tort that caused the damage had not been committed.[531]

*293.* Article 1787 of the Civil Law, which sets the rules for the calculation of lost profits, states that this type of damages must be proven to a level that would be credible as legal evidence that such detriment resulted. Under Article 1787 of the Civil Law, the court has no right to determine lost profit of its own accord (in Latin:

527. Torgāns, K. Komentārs Civillikuma 1771.pantam [*Commentary of Article 1771 of the Civil Law*]. Grām.: Latvijas Republikas Civillikuma komentāri. Ceturtā daļa. Saistību tiesības [*Commentary to the Civil Law of the Republic of Latvia. The fourth part. Law of Obligations*]. (2000), 268.lpp.
528. Torgāns, K. (2018), *supra* n. 11, 204–205.lpp. With reference to: Kalniņš, V. Romiešu civiltiesību pamati [*Basics of Roman Civil Law*]. Rīga: Izdevniecība 'Zvaigzne', 1977, 172.lpp.
529. Kalniņš E. Jēdziena 'zaudējumi' izpratnes tālākas attīstīšanas nepieciešamība [*The Need to Further Develop the Understanding of the Concept of 'Damages'*]. Latvijas Republikas Satversmei – 95. Latvijas Universitātes 75.zinātniskās konferences rakstu krājums [*For the 95th anniversary of the Constitution of the Republic of Latvia – the collection of writings of the 75th Scientific Conference of the University of Latvia*]. Rīga: LU Akadēmiskais apgāds, 2017, 57.lpp.
530. Kubilis, J. (2016), *supra* n. 78, 123.lpp.
531. Kalniņš, E. (2017), *supra* n. 529, 58–59.lpp.

*sua sponte* or *suo motu*) or to presume it.[532] As to aspects of proving and calculating lost profits, the Supreme Court has acknowledged that the claimant has to prove the fact that profit was lost due to the tortfeasor's actions. In addition, it is important to be able to prove that there is a real margin of profit, for which any legal means of proof can be used.[533]

*294.* It has been stated in court practice that lost profit is a quantity that characterizes reduction of profit with sufficient certainty due to a wrongful act. When examining the calculation of expected profit, the court must assess the evidence that supports it, including accounting documents. A determination of the amount of lost profits is mainly based on economic calculations. In order to determine the expected profit margin, it is not necessary to analyse the already realized economic activity of the victim, but planned and unrealized economic activity, taking into account various factors that might have affected the profit and the particular market itself. The final result when calculating lost profit should consist of income obtained from the sale of a product after deduction of taxes and other costs necessary for the acquisition and sale of the final product.[534]

*295.* Some exceptions from the principles of proof of lost profit are set in other legal acts. For example, Article 69.[1] (1) of the Copyright Law states that if objects of copyright or related rights have been illegally used due to a person's fault, the right-holders of copyright and related rights are entitled to require compensation of pecuniary and non-pecuniary damage. The victim is entitled to lost profits as well. If the amount of lost profits cannot be determined in line with the Civil Law, the amount will be determined according to the amount which, at the discretion of a court, could be received by the holders of copyright and related rights if the wrongful act had not occurred. Another exception is included in the Competition Law, whose Article 21(1) states that a victim who has suffered damage due to an infringement of Competition Law is entitled to compensation by way of damages from the tortfeasor, including lost profit. However, Article 21(3) of the Competition Law states that if the infringement is a cartel agreement, it is presumed that the price has been raised by 10% and that is the amount of lost profits unless the tortfeasor proves otherwise (*see also* paragraphs 308 and 309 *infra*).

## §6. Other Costs: Costs of Assessing Damages and Liability; Costs of Obtaining Judicial or Extra-Judicial Payment

*296.* The costs of assessing damages and liability as well as costs of obtaining judicial payment are not compensable as damages. Legal costs, including a notary's legal assistance in the preparation of procedural documents, cannot be qualified as

532. Torgāns, K.; Kārkliņš, J.; Bitāns, A. (2017), *supra* n. 70, 283–284.lpp.
533. Judgment of the Supreme Court of 14 Sep. 2018 in Case No. SKC-245/2018 (C20186514), point 15.2.
534. Judgment of the Supreme Court of 27 May. 2020 in Case No. SKC-309/2020 (C24044908), point 11.

damages and cannot be compensated based on Article 1635 of the Civil Law. The costs to be reimbursed in civil proceedings are governed by Chapter 4 of the CPL, in which Article 44 constitutes an exhaustive determination of the costs related to proceedings and reimbursement thereof. Under Article 44(1)(1) of that Law, only expenditure for payment of assistance by an advocate will be reimbursed.[535]

*297.* Under Article 44(2) of the CPL, recovery of expenses related to conducting a case will be ordered in favour of a wholly or partially successful claimant against the defendant. Under Article 33(3) of the CPL, expenses related to conducting a case are: (1) expenses for assistance from advocates; (2) expenses related to attending court hearings; (3) expenses related to gathering evidence; (4) expenses for state-assured legal aid; (5) expenses for the assistance of an interpreter at a court hearing. In short, the victim of a tort may claim not only damages but also the costs of the proceedings. If compensation for damage caused is compensated, then the expenses related to conducting a case are limited by the CPL.

*298.* Article 44(1) of the CPL regulates the amounts of expenses related to conducting a case:

Expenses for the assistance of an advocate:

(1) reimbursable expenses for paying for the assistance of an advocate in claims not exceeding EUR 8,500 – in the actual amount but not exceeding 30% of the satisfying part of the claim;
(2) reimbursable expenses for paying for the assistance of an advocate in claims from EUR 8,501 to EUR 57,000 – in the actual amount but not exceeding EUR 2,850;
(3) reimbursable expenses for paying for the assistance of an advocate in claims exceeding EUR 57,001 – in the actual amount but not exceeding 5% of the satisfying part of the claim.

*299.* Travel and accommodation expenses related to attending a court hearing:

- in accordance with the rates stipulated by the Government for reimbursing official travel expenses.

Expenses related to obtaining documentary evidence:

- the actual amount of expenses.

Expenses for an interpreter:

- in the amount for actual expenses but not more than the rates set by the Cabinet.

535. Judgment of the Supreme Court of 30 Oct. 2015 in Case No. SKC-224/2015 (C27215412), point 8.

*300*. Certain procedures must also be followed when in addition to damages the victim claims the expenses mentioned above. The Supreme Court acknowledges that if a party has not applied for the recovery of trial-related expenses under Article 44 of the CPL these claims cannot be brought later in a separate case.[536]

*301*. It should be added that when determining the exact amount to be reimbursed for the assistance of an advocate, the court may also decide on a reduction of the amount. However, under Article 44(5) of the CPL, the court may decide to set a smaller amount for reimbursable advocate's assistance at the initiative of a party to the case. The court may rule on the matter of its own accord only if there is a special exception to the principles of disposition and adversarial proceedings, which the court must state the reasons for.[537]

### §7. Mitigation of Damages

*302*. Article 1776 of the Civil Law requires the victim to reduce the damage caused to them. This Article refers to Article 1646 of the Civil Law, which states that a victim must act as a prudent and careful person or take such measures as a reasonable person would take in a particular situation to mitigate damages. Reasonable measures must be assessed in the light of the circumstances of the case (such as the time when activities were carried out or the possibility of concluding new contracts) and the reasonable person test, that is to say, whether a reasonable person would do the same in those circumstances.[538] However, not all agreements that mitigate damages are legally allowed by the Civil Law. Under Article 1643 of the Civil Law, any previous agreement not to compensate damages from an act committed with wrongful intent is void. However, the victim may waive a claim regarding a wrongful act if sufficiently informed about both the claim and the basis for it.

*303*. The purpose of Article 1776 of the Civil Law is to prevent the passivity of a victim who could prevent or reduce damages. The victim cannot be required to take additional time-consuming or costly measures, but damages should be mitigated if reasonably possible. Measures taken by the victim may be aimed at both reducing risk and avoiding damages in the event of a wrongful act.[539] An exception to this provision should only be allowed in the event of a malicious infringement of rights.[540] Under Article 1776(2) of the Civil Law, in a case of malicious infringement of rights, the victim's behaviour does not matter at all.[541]

536. Judgment of the Supreme Court of 6 Apr. 2011 in Case No. SKC-143/2011, point 7.
537. Judgment of the Supreme Court of 4 Nov. 2020 in Case No. SKC-974/2020 (C12193319), point 8.3.
538. Torgāns, K.; Kārkliņš, J.; Bitāns, A. (2017), *supra* n. 70, 235.lpp.
539. *Ibid.*, 234.lpp.
540. Judgment of the Supreme Court of 16 Jun. 2021 in Case No. SKC-216/2021 (C30596617), point 8.3.2.
541. Judgment of the Supreme Court of 17 Nov. 2016 in Case No. SKC-309/2016 (C32368111), point 8.1.

## Chapter 3. Assessment and Compensation of Damages

*304.* As mentioned earlier, an opinion is expressed in Latvian civil-law literature that the difference theory (*Differenztheorie*), recognized in German and Swiss civil law, may be exploited to explain the diminution of property being at the heart of the concept of damages. Therefore damages in Latvian law means the difference between (1) the actual condition (value) of an injured person's property after an illegal action, that caused the damage, was committed and (2) the hypothetical value of the injured person's property which would be the case if no tort had been committed or the debtor had properly performed their contractual obligations.[542] This corresponds to the explanation of damages given earlier, namely that damages means any increase of property, loss and harm to it, lost profit, additional expenses and other monetary consequences of a violation of rights.[543] Damages may manifest themselves not only as a decrease in assets but also as an increase in liabilities.[544] This approach applies not only in civil-law disputes but also in other areas of law. Thus, in an administrative case, where a person appealed against a factual action by the prison administration, the Supreme Court referred to the findings of

*305.* legal doctrine and on that basis ruled that the state must compensate the costs of the applicant's legal assistance in a situation where an invoice had been delivered but not yet paid.[545]

### §1. Objective Versus Subjective

*306.* The law is basically concerned that the amount of damages should correspond to the victim's actual loss with the purpose of restoring the victim to the position in which they would be if the violation had not occurred. Therefore the amount should objectively cover the amount of the victim's lost assets or increased liabilities and to a certain extent it should also cover subjective value lost due to the particular tort. Hence the law provides that assessing particular property (i.e., damage done to it) requires consideration not only of its normal value but also its special value to the injured party. However, value based only on personal inclinations does not need to be considered.[546] Legal doctrine provides several examples regarding the assessment of this special or, at least to some extent, subjective value. For example, if the owner had a retro writing machine, which was particularly adjusted for its particular user and this machine is destroyed due to a tort, the amount of damages to be compensated should be larger than the average cost of a similar writing

542. Kalniņš, E. (2017), *supra* n. 529, 61.lpp.
543. Torgāns, K. [*Commentary of Article 1770 of the Civil Law*], grām.: Latvijas Republikas Civillikuma komentāri. Saistību tiesības (1401–2400.p.) [*Commentary to the Civil Law of the Republic of Latvia. Law of Obligations (Arts 1401–2400)*]. (2000), 267.lpp.
544. Kalniņš, E. (2017), *supra* n. 529, 61.lpp.
545. Judgment of the Supreme Court of 23 Sep. 2019 in Case No. SKA-131/2019. Available at https://www.at.gov.lv/lv/tiesu-prakse/judikaturas-nolemumu-arhivs/administrativo-lietu-departaments/hronologiska-seciba?lawfilter=0&year=2019 [accessed on 30 Nov. 2021].
546. Article 1789 CL.

machine.[547] Also, if the violin of a professional violinist is destroyed due to a tort, the amount of damages may include not only the value of the destroyed violin but also lost profit, taking into account that the violinist may not be able to perform for some time.[548] However, if the violinist inherited the violin from their father, who was also a famous violinist, the amount of damages may not reflect this personal bond.[549]

## §2. Concrete Versus Abstract

*307.* The law usually requires that the amount of damages should be calculated precisely in line with the value of certain property, other loss inflicted indirectly by the event that caused damage, and lost profit.[550] Specifically in the case of tort the amount of damages will be calculated according to the value of the property concerned at the moment when the tort occurred.[551] The Supreme Court emphasized the necessity for a link between the amount of damages and the value of the affected property in a case where the court examined a claim for compensation of damage for a flooded residential apartment in a multi-apartment building.[552]

*308.* However, in certain categories of case the amount of damages may be calculated according to some presumption specified in the law, or according to other, rather abstract criteria.

*309.* If damage is caused by a breach of competition law, and it is not possible to accurately determine an amount of damages, the court may determine the amount of damages abstractly, but taking into account the extent of possible conclusions regarding certain damages, expenses and other relevant aspects arising from the evidence in the particular case.[553] In line with settled court practice, this rather abstract calculation of the amount of damages is allowed only if an accurate calculation of damages in the given case is not possible. The claimant is not allowed to choose between the accurate or abstract calculation of damages.[554]

547. Torgāns, K. [Commentary of Article 1789 of the Civil Law], grām.: Latvijas Republikas Civillikuma komentāri. Saistību tiesības (1401–2400.p.) [*Commentary to the Civil Law of the Republic of Latvia. Law of Obligations (Arts 1401–2400)*]. (2000), 278.lpp.
548. Буковский, В. (1914), *supra* n. 150, c.1410.
549. The example provided in the context with explanation given by the following source: Torgāns K. [Commentary of Article 1789 of the Civil Law], grām.: Latvijas Republikas Civillikuma komentāri. Saistību tiesības (1401–2400.p.) [*Commentary to the Civil Law of the Republic of Latvia. Law of Obligations (Arts 1401–2400)*]. (2000), 278.lpp.
550. Article 1786 CL.
551. Article 1792 CL.
552. Judgment of the Supreme Court of 26 Jan. 2011 in Case No. SKC-40/2011. Available at https://www.at.gov.lv/lv/tiesu-prakse/judikaturas-nolemumu-arhivs/civillietu-departaments/hronologiska-seciba?lawfilter=0&year=2011 [accessed on 30 Nov. 2021].
553. Article 21(1) Competition Law.
554. Judgment of the Supreme Court of 9 Apr. 2019 in Case No. SKC-94/2019. Available at https://www.at.gov.lv/lv/tiesu-prakse/judikaturas-nolemumu-arhivs/civillietu-departaments/hronologiska-seciba?lawfilter=0&year=2019 [accessed on 30 Nov. 2021].

*310.* As we have seen (paragraph 237 *supra*) the Competition Law provides one more rather abstract assumption of the amount of damages. Namely, in the case of a cartel agreement, it is presumed that the price of goods or services received was increased by 10%, which the recipient of goods or services may claim as damages. The seller or provider of services, however, is entitled to prove that the price increase was smaller or perhaps, in the particular case, does not exist at all.[555] In other words, the law in this situation provides a rebuttable presumption.

*311.* If the tax authority – the State Revenue Service – has wrongly collected a tax payment, the taxpayer is entitled to repayment of the wrongly collected amount plus half of that amount for the delay. If tax authority does not timely return the wrongly collected tax payment, the amount may be amended even further.[556] In this respect, the Supreme Court has clarified that these amounts, which should be added to wrongly collected tax payments, are in essence compensation for lost profit. However, in cases when the law provides the taxpayer with the right to receive these additional amounts, the taxpayer is released from the general requirement under Article 1787 of the Civil Law to prove lost profits at least to the level of credible legal evidence.[557]

*312.* A user of natural gas must compensate for damage caused by using gas without a commercial meter or a damaged meter, due to which the measurements of gas actually used are decreased or enabled the use of gas without payment. The amount of damages in this case will be calculated according to the amount of gas, determined according to the amount used in similar circumstances within a similar period or according to norms of annual and monthly consumption specified for households.[558]

*313.* If a tort has caused death or injury, the amount of non-pecuniary damage which the person liable for the tort must compensate to the victim or the victim's relatives will be decided at the discretion of the court.[559] Details of how this amount should be calculated are examined in Chapter 4 *infra*.

## §3. Methods of Assessing Damages

*314.* The purpose of compensation of damages is *restitutio in integrum* or, in other words, to return a person who has suffered damages to the situation (or at least the possibly closest situation) in which they would have been if the violation that

555. Article 21(3) Competition Law.
556. Article 28(1) and (2) the Law on Taxes and Fees.
557. Judgment of the Supreme Court of 1 Feb. 2013 in Case No. SKA-95/2013. Available at https://www.at.gov.lv/lv/tiesu-prakse/judikaturas-nolemumu-arhivs/administrativo-lietu-departaments/hronologiska-seciba?lawfilter=0&year=2013 [accessed on 30 Nov. 2021].
558. Points 87 and 88 of Cabinet Regulations No. 78 of 7 Feb. 2017 'Regulations Regarding the Trade and Use of Natural Gas'.
559. Article 2347(1) CL.

caused the damage had not occurred.[560] Therefore the methods applied in order to reach this objective must be appropriate for that purpose. Also, in assessing the amount of pecuniary damages, the chosen method must properly reflect the difference between (1) the actual condition (value) of the injured person's property after the illegal act that caused the damage, and (2) the hypothetical value of the injured person's property if the particular tort had not been committed.

*315.* Apart from situations where the law prescribes certain presumptions as described in the previous paragraph, the law does not explicitly specify methods for assessment of damages. Therefore, victims may use any appropriate method, starting from a simple comparison but also including sophisticated calculations in order to assess damages, as far as the chosen method is in line with the purpose of compensating damages.

*316.* The law refers only to the usual and special value of property to be taken into account during the assessment of damages if the damage appears to have decreased the value of the property.[561] The special value of property should reflect the special relation of the owner to their property (for example, the importance of a violin to a professional violinist, as mentioned above), but should not refer to any sentimental affection *(pretium affectionis)* of the owner towards their property.[562]

*317.* Legal scholar and practitioner Dr iur. Kubilis has correctly asserted that assessment of the value of property cannot be based only on its market value and should take into account other aspects, such as fluctuations in this value over time and the costs of liquidating the consequences of infringement.[563] These findings correspond to the opinion of another legal scholar and practitioner, Dr iur. Kalniņš, who has validly emphasized that in the case of damage to property, the amount of damages which the person liable has to compensate to the owner should be equal to the costs necessary to return the damaged property to its previous condition.[564] The amount of these costs may also exceed the market value of the property.

*318.* Some words have to be said about anticipated future loss. The wording of the law suggests that where damages are anticipated but have not yet appeared, the person about to face these damages may claim security (for example, in the form of interim measures) from the person liable.[565] However, as follows from recent court practice and legal doctrine, this wording may provide a somewhat misleading impression that a person is not allowed to claim damages before they have fully materialized.

560. Torgāns, K. (2018.), *supra* n. 11, 199.lpp.
561. Articles 871 and 872 CL.
562. Буковскій, В. (1914), *supra* n. 150, c.273.
563. Kubilis, J. (2016), *supra* n. 78, 112–113.lpp.
564. Kalniņš, E. (2017), *supra* n. 529, 55.lpp.
565. Article 1771 CL.

*319.* The Supreme Court has ruled that if damages include loss of income, which is certainly anticipated, the person entitled to this income can claim its loss as damages even though they have not yet materialized.[566]

*320.* As we have seen, opinion in Latvian legal doctrine suggests that damages include not only decrease in assets but also increase in liabilities. Therefore, an injured person who is about to face certain expenses but has not yet covered them is entitled to claim these expenses from the person liable. Hence assessment of damages in such situations should cover this anticipated but not yet materialized income and expenses.[567]

## §4. Equitable Limitation of Damage

*321.* Equitable limitation of damage is regulated differently for pecuniary and for non-pecuniary damage.

*322.* As regards pecuniary damage, the law entitles a person liable to claim a reduction in the amount of damages which the victim could have avoided by exercising reasonable measures for mitigation of damages.[568] For further details on mitigation of damages, *see* Part IV Chapter 2, section 7 *infra*.

*323.* Regarding non-pecuniary damage, the law does not have explicit provisions on equitable limitation of damage. However, this does not mean that such limitation does not exist. Indeed, it can be derived from the principle of good faith under Article 1 of the Civil Law, which prevents inappropriate use of rights[569] or, to be more precise, use of rights to claim non-pecuniary damage in order to achieve enrichment, seek vengeance or to pursue another target, which according to law is not a target for compensation of non-pecuniary damage or is not a legitimate purpose at all.

*324.* The aspect of equitable limitation of damage had particular importance after the so-called Zolitude tragedy that took place on 21 November 2013, when in the result of collapse of a supermarket roof fifty-four people were killed and several dozens were injured.[570] This tragic event was followed by several lawsuits claiming compensation for deceased and injured victims. These claims were specific with the amount of compensation claimed, which reached around 70 million EUR for every deceased person, thus many times exceeding the amounts granted in settled court practice and in more detail analysed in Chapter 4 *infra*. The amounts claimed were

566. Judgment of the Supreme Court of 15 Jan. 2014 in Case No. SKC-12/2014. Available at https://www.at.gov.lv/lv/tiesu-prakse/judikaturas-nolemumu-arhivs/civillietu-departaments/hronologiska-seciba?lawfilter=0&year=2014 [accessed on 01 Dec. 2021].
567. Kalniņš, E. (2017), *supra* n. 529, 57.lpp.
568. Article 1776(2) CL.
569. Balodis, K. (2007), *supra* n. 69, 143.lpp.
570. *https://www.la.lv/publisko-zolitude-bojagajuso-personu-sarakstu-bernu-taja-nav* [accessed on 1 Dec. 2021].

criticized by Torgāns, who validly emphasized that the purpose of compensation for non-pecuniary damage is not to provide the victim with financial means which they could not achieve if the tort had not happened. Torgāns compared these amounts with amounts awarded in other European countries. According to this comparison, 600,000 EUR is the highest average amount granted in Germany.[571] This approach corresponds to the writings of other authors, namely that the object of tort law (and hence the compensation awarded) is also limited to achieving *restitution in integrum* and, therefore, the general rule is that payments made to the victim that are intended as a substitute for damages, and which are awarded in respect of an identical loss, are deductible, for example, payments under insurance schemes.[572]

## §5. Methods of Payment

### I. Lump Sum

*325.* A lump sum is a general method of compensating pecuniary as well as non-pecuniary damage in Latvian practice and Latvian court practice. Other methods could be awarded only in cases where, for some valid reason, a lump sum award is not a feasible option.

### II. Annuities

*326.* Annuities may be awarded in the case of personal injury and death if determination of a lump sum is either not possible (for example, if the period in which the person who was under the deceased victim's custody will gain the possibility to earn the means of living by themself could not be foreseen in advance) or will create an impossible burden for the person liable in damages for example if lost income over several years has to be compensated. Thus, for instance, where due to injury, the victim is permanently unable to continue their occupation from which they earned a living, the person liable must compensate them for lost income in the form of an annuity.[573] If in the result of a tort, someone dies who has a duty to maintain some other person, then the person liable for the death of the deceased person has to compensate for maintenance costs, a duty that also may be expressed in the form of annuity payments.[574]

571. Torgāns, K. Atbildības par morālo kaitējumu aktualitātes. *[Urgent Issues of Liability for Moral Damage]* In: Tiesību efektīvas piemērošanas problemātika. Latvijas Universitātes 72. zinātniskās konferences rakstu krājums. Rīga: LU Akadēmiskais apgāds, 2014, 134–135.lpp.
572. Van Dam, C. (2013), *supra* n. 332, pp. 372–373.
573. Article 2348 CL.
574. Article 2351 CL.

## III. Other

*327.* Compensation in the form of payment method other than lump sum and annuity is very rare in Latvian practice. However, such a possibility might arise if there are valid reasons for it. For example, the court has ordered a construction company to compensate damages to a customer caused by poor workmanship by means of paying the respective amount of money into the deposit account of the bailiff in order to be released when the bailiff is presented with a document for payment of construction works and materials necessary to fix the defects omitted by the defendant construction company.[575]

575. Judgment of Vidzeme Regional Court of 6 Oct. 2015 in Case No. C33554112 (CA-0225-15/14). Not published.

# Chapter 4. Personal Injury and Death

## §1. Pecuniary Damage

*328.* If a tort causes death or bodily injury to another person, the tortfeasor should compensate various pecuniary damages to the victim or their relatives:

(a) First of all, the tortfeasor must compensate the victim's costs of medical treatment, including rehabilitation. This includes the duty to compensate these expenses if the victim has died.[576]
(b) Also, as already mentioned, if the injury made the victim unable to continue their occupation from which they earned their living, whether for a certain time or permanently, the tortfeasor must compensate the victim's lost income.[577]
(c) If a tort caused the victim's death, the tortfeasor will have to compensate the expenses of the victim's funeral.[578]
(d) In addition, if a deceased victim had a duty to maintain some other person, then the person liable for the death of the victim must compensate the maintenance expenses of the dependant person.[579]

## §2. Non-pecuniary Damage

*329.* In the case of bodily injury, the victim is entitled to compensation by way of non-pecuniary damage, including compensation for mutilation or disfigurement in appropriate cases.[580] In the case of a victim's death, their relatives are entitled to receive compensation for their loss as well.[581]

*330.* A person is entitled to compensation for non-pecuniary damage if illegally deprived of their freedom.[582] This provision also applies where someone was deprived of their freedom in the result of detention, which later turned out to be unfounded, i.e., if the court finds that person not guilty or the criminal investigation against that person is terminated on exonerating grounds.[583]

*331.* A person is entitled to compensation for non-pecuniary damage if their reputation and dignity are injured by published information, verbal statements or acts.[584]

576. Articles 1635, 2347(1) and 2350 CL.
577. Articles 2347(1) and 2348 CL.
578. Article 2350 CL.
579. Article 2351 CL.
580. Articles 2347 (1) and 2349 CL.
581. Article 1635 CL.
582. Article 2352 CL.
583. Article 8(1) Law on Compensation of Damages, caused by State Authorities (*Valsts pārvaldes iestāžu nodarīto zaudējumu atlīdzības likums*).
584. Article 2352.[1] CL.

*332.* A person is entitled to compensation in the case of non-consensual sexual intercourse.[585]

*333.* In all these situations, compensation is assessed at the discretion of the court. Both legal doctrine and court practice provide several criteria to be taken into account when assessing compensation for non-pecuniary damage.

*334.* It should be kept in mind that not every item of damage entitles the person who suffered harm through some unpleasant situation or feelings to claim damage for it. The right to claim compensation is attributable only to cases of legally relevant damage exceeding the borders of the usual risks of life. For instance, an eyewitness to a terrible accident is not entitled to claim compensation as a result, even though they may have disturbing memories and feelings afterwards.[586] In other words, Latvian tort law does not guarantee that people will not experience such situations and hence there is also no remedy in the form of compensation.

*335.* Although compensation of non-pecuniary damage also has the objective of *restitutio in integrum*, assessing it is more complicated in comparison with cases of pure pecuniary damage. Therefore, Latvian legal doctrine has developed several functions which are specific for non-pecuniary damage and have to be taken into account in assessment of non-pecuniary damage. These functions are (1) conciliation, i.e., the amount of compensation aims to diminish the victim's suffering and help them to accept the fact and leave it in the past; (2) fairness, i.e., the amount of compensation must be considered fair from the reasonable perspective of both parties; (3) prevention, i.e., it aims to deter the person liable and other persons in general from committing such and similar deeds in future.[587] Although this is not very much emphasized or analysed in Latvian legal doctrine and court practice, the important question could be whether all three functions are relevant where non-pecuniary damage is to be compensated on the basis of strict liability without fault. Namely, debate could arise about whether the preventive function is relevant, as in reality, there may be no future faulty activity or inactivity to be prevented. It is also important to emphasize that the preventive function does not mean that compensation may be applied as a punishment: This is neither possible nor acceptable under Latvian law.[588]

*336.* These functions provide certain guidelines on the assessment of the amount of compensation for non-pecuniary damage. However, this assessment is still a rather complicated enterprise. Therefore, even more important to these functions is the comparative method, providing that in similar situations, similar compensation should be awarded. In order to make the application of the comparative method easier, the Supreme Court has published a survey on court practice in assessing

585. Article 2353 CL.
586. Torgāns, K.; Kārkliņš, J.; Bitāns, A. (2017), *supra* n. 70, 272–273.lpp.
587. *Ibid.*, 279.lpp.
588. *Ibid.*, 282.lpp.

compensation for infringement of a claimant's rights, bodily injury or loss of a relative. According to the survey, the highest amount of compensation is around EUR 142,000 granted in the case of severe injuries causing the disability of the claimant for their entire life.[589] However, in this case, the court made an interesting remark, namely that the rather high amount also covered compensation to the mother and brother of the injured victim. This aspect has not been substantially analysed in subsequent court practice, although it might be that in certain cases, severe injury to the person causes non-pecuniary damage to their relatives.

*337.* Court practice also sets certain limits on who is entitled to claim damages when someone dies in the result of a tort. The court referred to Article 19 of the Annex to Resolution (75) 7 of 14 March 1975 of the Council of Europe Cabinet of Ministers on Compensation for Physical Injury or Death, stating that the circle of possible claimants should not extend beyond the spouse of the victim and their children, parents and fiancée, if they had a close bond of affection to the victim. On this ground, brothers and sisters of a deceased victim are usually not entitled to claim compensation. Also, the usual approach of the court is that the relatives of a deceased person are entitled to one amount for the death of their relative.[590] If the tort appeared in the form of a criminal offence against someone's life, health, morals, sexual integrity, liberty, honour, dignity or family, or against a minor, it is presumed that the victim has suffered moral harm as a result of the act. However, this does not mean that in every case, the claimant must prove the existence of non-pecuniary damage in the same way as required for proving pecuniary damage. This may be replaced with reasonable assessment by the court or even the court may apply a reversed burden of proof. Thus, in one case, a detainee filed a claim against the police for compensation for non-pecuniary damage caused by a situation where letters that the detainee wrote to his wife were opened, checked and even commented on by the police. The police tried to argue that the claimant had not proved that their actions caused damage. However, the court emphasized that in such a case, it should be assumed that it is the duty of the defendant to prove that it has a legally valid reason to control the correspondence of detainees and in the given case the defendant had failed to demonstrate any such legally valid reasons and so it could be concluded that the defendant had committed an infringement. At the same time, the question remains whether the consequences of infringement were so harsh that they entitled the claimant to compensation. This aspect must be proved by the claimant.[591]

---

589. Latvijas Republikas Augstākā tiesa. Tiesu prakse morālā kaitējuma apmēra noteikšanā saistībā ar prasītājam nodarīto tiesību aizskārumu, miesas bojājumiem vai tuvinieka bojāeju *[Court practice on assessment of amount of the compensation for the infringement to the rights of claimant, bodily injury or loss of relative]*, 2016., 32.lpp. Available at https://www.at.gov.lv/lv/tiesu-prakse/tiesu-prakses-apkopojumi/civiltiesibas [accessed on 2 Dec. 2021].

590. Latvijas Republikas Augstākā tiesa. Morālā kaitējuma atlīdzināšana civillietās. *[Compensation of non-pecuniary damage in civil cases].* Tiesu prakses apkopojums, 2014, 46.lpp. Available at https://www.at.gov.lv/lv/tiesu-prakse/tiesu-prakses-apkopojumi/civiltiesibas [accessed on 2 Dec. 2021].

591. *Ibid.*, 42.lpp.

*338.* In a case where someone was imprisoned for three years on grounds which later proved unfounded, the court awarded compensation for non-pecuniary damage of EUR 7,000. It also took into account that the length of criminal proceedings in total was six years and additional measures, such as police monitoring, were applied. In a case where someone was accused of a serious criminal offence on the grounds that later proved unfounded, the amount of compensation for non-pecuniary damage was EUR 1,000. This amount was awarded taking into account that the entire criminal proceedings lasted for three years, although no detention was involved.[592]

*339.* If a claimant files a claim for compensation of non-pecuniary damage because of publication of certain information, the court will assess four criteria: (1) whether the information was published, not just disclosed in private; however, it is sufficient if this information was disclosed at least to one more person in addition to the claimant, (2) information has to be disclosed as factual information, not as mere opinion; (3) the information must be harmful to the honour and dignity of the person concerned; (4) whether the defendant proves that the information under question is true. [593] One of the most interesting criteria among these four is the criterion of being information presented as not a mere opinion. In general, reputation and dignity may be harmed only by information which is not true. Hence, if the information is not true (and the other three criteria are met), the claimant may be awarded compensation. A mere opinion could not be either true or wrong and in general may not provide a ground for awarding compensation by way of non-pecuniary damage.[594] However, there are also two exceptions.

*340.* First, in exceptional cases, if the opinion lacks any factual basis and is provided in an extremely rude, harsh or otherwise aggressive manner, it may also cause civil liability for non-pecuniary damage. The question of whether the opinion lacks any factual ground and is expressed in an unacceptable manner will be assessed according to the context which, and how, the opinion was expressed.[595]

*341.* Second, in exceptional cases, publication of true information may give a reason for civil liability for non-pecuniary damage. In order to determine whether publication of the information amounts to a good reason, the court will assess five criteria, stemming from the court practice of the Court of Justice of the European

592. Latvijas Republikas Augstākā tiesa. Tiesu prakse morālā kaitējuma apmēra noteikšanā, ja kaitējums radies izziņas iestādes, prokuratūras vai tiesas nelikumīgas vai nepamatotas rīcības gadījumā. *[Court practice on assessment of amount of compensation for non-pecuniary* damage, *if the damage is caused in the result of illegal or ungrounded action of investigation authority, prosecutor's office or court].* (Tiesu prakse 2007–2016.), 2016, 8.lpp. Available at https://www.at.gov.lv/lv/tiesu-prakse/tiesu-prakses-apkopojumi/civiltiesibas [accessed on 2 Dec. 2021].

593. Latvijas Republikas Augstākā tiesa. Goda un cieņas civiltiesiskā aizsardzība. *[Protection of reputation and dignity from the perspective of civil law].* Tiesu prakses apkopojums. (2000–2021.gada maijs). 4.lpp. Available at https://www.at.gov.lv/lv/tiesu-prakse/tiesu-prakses-apkopojumi/civiltiesibas [accessed on 2 Dec. 2021].

594. *Ibid.*, 8.lpp.

595. Torgāns, K.; Kārkliņš, J.; Bitāns, A. (2017), *supra* n. 70, 347–348.lpp.

Union: (1) the importance of the information to the public, i.e., whether the information satisfied certain public needs or simply satisfied the mere curiosity of some people; (2) whether the information refers to a publicly well-known person and whether the information itself has public relevance or is strictly private; this means that the level of protection for publicly well-known individuals is lower, although even they are entitled to protect their strictly private information; (3) previous actions by the person who suffered the infringement, i.e., whether this person has already previously published some related information by themself or could have take steps in order to prevent potential or actual damage; (4) the manner in which the information was published and the means by which it was acquired, i.e., whether it was acquired lawfully; (5) the substance, form and consequences of publishing the information, i.e., whether it is possible to identify a certain person in the published information; the scope of the public reached by the information; whether publication affected the privacy of the person concerned.[596]

*342.* Similarly to other European countries, Latvian law enables natural persons and legal entities to claim compensation by way of non-pecuniary damage, emphasizing, however, that usually, the reputation of a legal entity will be assessed from the perspective of its commercial value, unless it includes any particular personal aspects. That is, the Supreme Court has established that the court will assess how the commercial value of the company name was affected due to the infringement; however, the personal feelings of the company representatives will not be taken into account.[597]

*343.* The defendants in claims are usually the entity which published the information. However, they may be co-defendants with a particular journalist or other author of the information. In that case, the court will separately assess the amount of liability of each defendant.[598]

*344.* Apart from the compensation for non-pecuniary damage, the claimant may also ask for revocation or amendment of the information. However, the fact that the claimant has not exercised their right to claim revocation or amendment of the information does not preclude them from the right to claim compensation.[599]

*345.* There is no standard amount of compensation, which hence should be assessed in each case separately according to the circumstances.[600]

596. Mālere, A. Patiesa informācija kā pamats personas reputācijas aizskārumam. *[True Information as a Ground for Infringement to the Reputation of the Persons].* Jurista Vārds, 2021, Nr.40, 24– 26., 29.lpp.
597. Latvijas Republikas Augstākā tiesa. Goda un cieņas civiltiesiskā aizsardzība. *[Protection of reputation and dignity from the perspective of civil law].* Tiesu prakses apkopojums. (2000–2021.gada maijs). 28.lpp. Available at https://www.at.gov.lv/lv/tiesu-prakse/tiesu-prakses-apkopojumi/civiltiesibas [accessed on 2 Dec. 2021].
598. *Ibid.,* 29–30.lpp.
599. *Ibid.,* 28.lpp.
600. *Ibid.,* 25.lpp.

## Chapter 5. Various Damages: Property

*346.* The Civil Law provides regulation if damages are caused to property as discussed above in this part of the monograph. A more complicated question is whether the Civil Law recognizes restitution in kind, i.e., restoration of an object damaged or destroyed by the tortfeasor. Both the concept of damages included in Article 1770 of the Civil Law and the basic norm for the duty of compensation of damages envisaged by Article 1779 of the Civil Law demonstrate that damages are closely linked with payment of money rather than the elimination of a deficiency in capacity that existed before the infringement. Likewise, restitution in kind is also not provided by Chapter 19 of the Law of Obligations Part of the Civil Law that contains rules for typical (i.e., listed) torts or quasi-torts. Indeed, the rules for compensation of pecuniary damage in torts refer either to general regulation of damages described above or provide compensation in money in the case of theft or robbery.[601] In this regard, Torgāns explains that such a link is provided simply because the same situation prevails in the case of a tort for damage to an object as in the cause of non-performance of contract.[602] Therefore, if an object is either destroyed or damaged, the victim cannot choose between restitution in kind or compensation of damages but is entitled to claim damages only, irrespective of the type of tort or conduct on the part of the tortfeasor or the degree of fault.

*347.* A specific rule is envisaged if a stolen object has been destroyed. In this case, the Civil Law provides a higher liability criterion than generally envisaged, i.e., compensation of the value of the object existing at the moment of occurrence of the damage as referred to in Article 1792 of the Civil Law.[603] In this situation, the victim may claim 'the highest price the property had from the time of the arbitrary taking'.[604]

601. Articles 2355–2357 CL.
602. Torgāns, K. (2018), *supra* n. 11, 489.lpp.
603. Bitāns, A. Komentārs Civillikuma 2356.pantam [Commentary of Article 2356 of the Civil Law]. Grām.: Latvijas Republikas Civillikuma komentāri: Ceturtā daļa. Saistību tiesības [*Commentary to the Civil Law of the Republic of Latvia: Part Four. Law of Obligations*]. (2000), 639.lpp.
604. Article 2356 CL.

# Chapter 6. Interference with Collateral Benefits

## §1. Insurance

*348.* An insurance contract is a well-recognized risk-shifting mechanism and is considered a universal legal instrument for compensation of damages in the result of occurrence of an insured risk under an insurance contract. Similarly to other European countries, Latvian insurance law distinguishes between voluntary insurance and compulsory insurance. This distinction is, however, provided in insurance supervision regulation, but it does not alter its contractual character. Indeed, Article 6 of the Insurance and Reinsurance Law explicitly states that insurance is voluntary, except for cases where the law prescribes otherwise.[605] Compulsory insurance is provided in Latvia only in civil liability insurance on the basis of separate legal acts in approximately twenty cases, including motor insurance, which is regulated by the Motor Insurance Law[606].[607]

*349.* Depending on the particular legal act, regulation on compulsory insurance may contain a procedure for submitting a claim by either the insured or the victim depending on whether a direct claim is allowed. The Insurance Contract Law[608] allows a direct claim if other legal acts so provide.[609] In this way, other legal acts allow a direct claim in two situations: one is motor insurance (referred to above) and the other is compulsory insurance of the civil liability of security merchants.[610] The latter situation is based on developments in Latvian court practice as no particular legal act explicitly allows a direct claim.[611]

*350.* Latvian tort law does not explicitly set a duty to reduce or reject a claim for compensation of damages if the insurance redress covers these damages partially or fully. However, this rule may be deduced from the very concept of damages that may be claimed in the case of diminution of property.[612] Therefore, if diminution of the property of the victim is partially or fully covered by the insurer, the victim is not allowed to claim damages in that part.

605. Insurance and Reinsurance Law. Official translation into English available on the official web-page of the State Language Centre at https://vvc.gov.lv/image/catalog/dokumenti/Insurance%20and%20Reinsurance%20Law.docx.
606. Compulsory Civil Liability Insurance of Owners of Motor Vehicles Law, *supra* n. 408.
607. Mantrov, V. *Insurance Law in Latvia*. AH Alphen aan den Rijn: Kluwer Law International, 2018, pp. 29–36.
608. Insurance Contract Law, *supra* n. 407.
609. *Ibid*, Art. 53.
610. Mantrovs, V. Apdrošināšanas tiesības [*Insurance Law*]. Rīga: LU Akadēmiskais apgāds, 2018, 190–192.lpp.
611. *Ibid.*
612. Article 1770 CL.

*351.* Likewise, a similar conclusion may be drawn from the perspective of an insurance contract if the victim has obtained compensation for damages from a tortfeasor or other sources.[613] Indemnity insurance covers property and civil liability insurance that prevents a claim for damages in a higher amount than damage actually caused. This rule is explained in Latvia in such a way that insurance redress under the indemnity insurance principle may not exceed losses caused in the insured event.[614] This means that if a tortfeasor has compensated damages partially or fully, this should be taken into account in providing insurance redress.

*352.* In motor insurance, a motor insurer or the Latvian national insurer bureau may claim insurance redress in part or in full if damages are covered by other sources. Indeed, the Motor Insurance Law states that:

> If an insurer or the Motor Insurers' Bureau has carried out the payment of an insurance indemnity but subsequently such facts have been established which were not known previously but would have been important in taking the decision to pay an insurance indemnity, the insurer or the Motor Insurers' Bureau has the right to request the beneficiary of the insurance indemnity to pay back the unjustifiably paid insurance indemnity or part of it on the basis of the right to reclaim laid down in the Civil Law.[615]

*353.* This relates only to indemnity insurance. A different approach should be taken in cases of insurance of fixed sums excluding health insurance (i.e., life and physical integrity in accident insurance) because the indemnity insurance principle is not applicable to that type of insurance. This means that if non-pecuniary damage is compensated by the tortfeasor or from other sources, the victim is still entitled to claim insurance redress from the insurer irrespective of the fact that compensation for non-pecuniary damage has already been received. This rule is under insurance contract regulation, although the insurance contract parties (actually the insurer) have a contractual choice to take into account compensation received from other sources or not.[616] However, this contractual choice is not possible in life insurance.[617]

## §2. Social Security

*354.* Separately from tort law falling within private law, Latvian social law provides for payment of allowances which could be used as compensation to victims in certain situations.

613. For other sources, *see* Sub-ch.3 of this Ch. *infra*.
614. Article 42(1) Insurance Contract Law, *supra* n. 407.
615. Article 41(5) Motor Insurance Law.
616. Article 55(3)–(4) Insurance Contract Law, *supra* n. 407.
617. *Ibid.*, Art. 55(4).

*355.* Latvian social law provides allowances in certain situations which may be invoked in the case of a tort. The Law On State Social Insurance[618] envisages the list of types of social security which includes, for example, social insurance against accidents at work and occupational diseases, and disability insurance, and health insurance. [619] The procedure for payment of allowances under these types of social security is laid down in other legal acts.

## §3. OTHER

*356.* It is possible that a victim receives compensation for damage from other sources than discussed in this chapter, that is, an insurance contract or social security. Two types of other such sources may be identified: either public or private sources.

*357.* As regards *public* sources, Latvian law is familiar with special regulation for compensation of victims of criminal offences. A victim (only in the capacity of a natural person) may claim compensation from the state for non-pecuniary damage, physical suffering or financial loss resulting from an intentional criminal offence on the basis of a separate legal act.[620] This does not clarify which part of the compensation refers to either pecuniary or non-pecuniary damage, but rather it is considered as a lump sum to be paid to the victim under the procedure laid down by that legal act. In order to be entitled to claim compensation, a person must be recognized as a victim in criminal proceedings, though it is not important whether a particular infringer has been identified or held criminally liable.[621] Yet this compensation cannot be claimed in the case of an offence in road traffic if the damage should be compensated within the motor insurance system.[622] There are set amounts of compensation depending on the type of damage, for instance, if someone has died – five minimum monthly wages determined at the time when the person was recognized as a victim (currently, the minimum monthly wage is set at 500 euro).[623] The deadline for claiming compensation is within three years from the day when a person has been recognized as a victim or has become aware of the facts that give them the right to be recognized as a victim.[624] If compensation is paid, the Legal Aid Administration (a state institution responsible for compensating victims under the discussed regulation) may claim repayment of compensation from a victim who knowingly provided false information in order to obtain state compensation or failed to provide certain information or a person admits liabilty for committing the offence.[625]

618. Law on State Social Insurance.
619. Article 4 Law on State Social Insurance.
620. Law on State Compensation to Victims.
621. Article 3(2) Law on State Compensation to Victims.
622. *Ibid.*, Art. 2(3).
623. *Ibid*, Art. 7.
624. *Ibid.*, Art. 9.
625. *Ibid.*, Art. 3.[1] (1) in conjuncture with Arts 19–25.

*358.* Also *private* sources are available for compensation of damage caused due to a tort when compensation is voluntarily provided by other persons due to the donation purpose.[626] For example, an employer agrees to compensate either fully or partially damage caused to an employee by a tortfeasor; or the next of kin agree to compensate damages due to kinship. Another example would be if an organization whose aim is to collect donations from members of the public is willing to donate in a particular case, fully or partially covers damages caused. For instance, the charity organization 'ziedot.lv' recently published a report stating that 407,020.25 EUR were donated to support victims of violence in the charity marathon Dod Pieci 2020.[627]

*359.* In this regard, the Administrative Regional Court, in reviewing a dispute over whether the state is under a duty to buy glasses for a prisoner concluded that:

> the state has the right to reduce the state budget expenditures as much as possible and, in situations where the purchase of specific medical devices is not intended to be covered from the state budget, to invite persons to use charity organizations and religious organizations. The activities and events organized by the charity organization 'Ziedot.lv' are widely known.[628]

*360.* Although this ruling was made in an administrative case and concerns expenditure for maintenance of prisoners, it can be applied generally by demonstrating that not only compensation of expenditure but also for damage may be sought from private sources as argued at the beginning of this paragraph.

*361.* In all these situations, the compensation received should be taken into account and lead to reduction of the amount of the claim or excluding a claim against the tortfeasor. An obstacle to this result could be if the tortfeasor is not aware of compensation of damages from other sources (especially in the case of both the above examples) that could remain unknown to public. Furthermore, an organization that compensates for damage through donations may bring a claim against the tortfeasor for compensation. However, none of these claims have been brought so far as the anonymized court practice database is concerned.

---

626. For a discussion of donation in Latvian civil law, *see* Torgāns, K.; Kārkliņš, J.; Mantrov, V.; Rasnačs, L., *supra* n. 4, pp. 272–278.
627. Ziedot.lv. Dod pieci 2020. Atskaite [report] 30 Nov. 2021. Available in Latvian at https://www.ziedot.lv/realizetie-projekti/dod-pieci-2020-3793/atskaite.
628. Judgment of Administrative Regional Court of 25 Nov. 2020 in Case A420236317 (not appealed; entered into force). Available in Latvian at https://manas.tiesas.lv/eTiesasMvc/nolemumi/pdf/432018.pdf.

# Chapter 7. Other Remedies

## §1. Restitution for Unjust Enrichment

*362.* The Civil Law provides different remedies concerning unjust enrichment and restitution after proof of unjust enrichment in addition to other remedies. Chapter 19 of the Law of Obligations Part of the Civil Law generally deals with unjust enrichment. Unjust enrichment occurs when someone keeps a thing – money, movables, immovables, even non-corporeal things, i.e., things without physical form – without lawful reason which allows the owner to reclaim it, i.e., claim restitution. It is not material whether no lawful reason existed or the item was later lost after being obtained, for instance, in the case of an invalid premature termination of a contract or theft (robbery).

*363.* Civil liability preconditions such as fault need not be established in order to have a claim for unjust enrichment and following restitution. Rather (depending on the ground for unjust enrichment, discussed *infra*), it is sufficient to establish certain set requirements in order to succeed with an unjust enrichment claim. At the same time, similarly as in the case of torts generally, the general limitation period of ten years applies to claims for unjust enrichment.[629]

*364.* Regulation of unjust enrichment and related restitution is based on ancient rules of Roman private law. This is why the Civil Law contains five unjust enrichment grounds which are very close to those which existed in Roman private law. These grounds must be employed in specific sequence. However, this conclusion is criticized for arguing that the fifth and final claim for unjust enrichment discussed below should be sufficient in any situation.[630] First of all, one should examine one of three grounds for unjust enrichment depending on specific preconditions to be established.[631] If none of them applies, the victim may use the right to reclaim on the grounds of absence of any legal basis.[632] However, this ground could be used only if a particular thing is at the disposal of the tortfeasor. If it has been transferred to some other person, then that person is responsible under the fifth and final ground for unjust enrichment: a general reclaim on the grounds of enrichment.[633]

## §2. Injunctive Relief

*365.* The Civil Law does not generally recognize the concept of injunctive relief for a claim to end an infringement. This conclusion is supported by Latvian civil-law literature which does not mention an injunction in the list of available remedies.[634]

629. Article 1895 CL.
630. Torgāns, K. (2018), *supra* n. 11, 501–502.lpp.
631. Articles 2369–2388 CL.
632. Article 2389–2390 CL.
633. Article 2391–2392 CL.
634. Torgāns, K. (2018), *supra* n. 11, 175–177.lpp.

*366.* At the same time, the Civil Law envisages separate provisions that may be used for injunctive relief, such as the right to self-defence. Indeed, Article 913 concerning interference with possession (*valdījums* in Latvian) provides that:

> Every person may protect his or her possession from any restriction or interference, even by force, provided that it is used without delay and within the limits permitted by law for justified self-defence.
> In this regard, a possessor may claim protection for their possession and also compensation for damages caused them through interference with their possession[635] as well as ask a court to require from the debtor a guarantee that such debtor will henceforth no longer interfere with possession.[636]

*367.* In a more uncertain formulation, Article 1040 of the Civil Law envisages a similar right for a proprietor by providing that:

> Owners have the right to self-defence and, in relation to this, even the right to destroy the property of other persons, due to which they should fear losing their own, if it is not possible for them to otherwise avert the threatened loss.

These provisions, however, relate to property and not to protection of lawful interests in general. This regulation is supplemented by a provision in the Law of Obligations Part that obligations rights, like all other private rights, may be protected only through the courts.[637]

*368.* At the same time, sui generis legal acts on intellectual property (and similar legal acts such as protection of trade secrets dealt with on the basis of *sui generis* regulation[638] based on an EU Directive[639]) are familiar with injunctions. These injunctions are based on substantive law but are simultaneously also provided at the procedural level as discussed below. For instance, under the newly adopted Trade Mark Law[640] an injunction order is a duty imposed by a court on an infringer to perform certain activities or to refrain from performing certain activities in order to end an infringement of the rights of a trade mark proprietor or to prevent a possible infringement [641]

635. Article 915 CL.
636. Article 916 CL.
637. Article 1732 CL.
638. Trade Secret Protection Law, *supra* n. 400.
639. Directive (EU) 2016/943 of the European Parliament and of the Council of 8 Jun. 2016 on the protection of undisclosed know-how and business information (trade secrets) against their unlawful acquisition, use and disclosure. OJ, L 157, 15.6.2016, pp. 1–18. For its implementation in Latvia, *see* Birstonas, R., Mantrov, V., Tavits, G., Kelli, A. Implementation of trade secrets directive in Baltic states: a step towards partial harmonization, in: Legal Science: Functions, Significance and Future in Legal Systems II: Collection of Research Papers in Conjunction with the 7th International Scientific Conference of the Faculty of Law of the University of Latvia, 16–18 Oct. 2019, Riga. Riga: University of Latvia, 2020, pp. 348–363. Available at https://www.apgads.lu.lv/fileadmin/user_upload/lu_portal/apgads/PDF/Juridiskas-konferences/ISCFLUL-7-2019/iscflul.7.2-28_Birstonas_Mantrovs_Tavits_Kelli.pdf.
640. Trade Mark Law. No English translation is available.
641. Article 55(1) Trade Mark Law.

*369.* Likewise, CPL generally[642] provides procedural rules for obtaining an injunction aimed at ending an infringement. *Two types* of injunction are distinguished: permanent (awarded by a court judgment when a case is reviewed on its merits) or temporary (interim), i.e., valid when the court proceedings are taking place or to be initiated.

*370.* The CPL provides a *permanent* injunction through a type of judgment imposing a duty to perform specific actions. Article 197(1) of the CPL states that:

> [i]n a judgment which imposes an obligation to perform specific actions, the court shall state specifically who is to perform them, what actions are to be performed and the time period within which they are to be performed.

However, if such a judgment is not fulfilled, the claimant is entitled to perform such actions at the expense of the defendant and thereafter recover payment of the necessary expenses from the defendant.[643]

*371.* A *temporary* (interim) injunction may be obtained through securing a claim as a specific civil procedure institute if enforcement of a court judgment may become problematic or impossible.[644] In this situation, a court or a judge may prohibit a defendant from performing certain actions as one of the means for securing a claim.[645]

*372.* In any of the above cases, an injunction may be sought independently from a claim for damages from the debtor. Likewise, awarding an injunction either of a substantive or procedural character is also related to establishing preconditions of civil liability.

## §3. Punitive Damages

*373.* Latvian civil law does not generally recognize the punitive function of tort law and therefore denies the availability of punitive damages. Similarly, the DCFR does not recognize punitive damages because they are inconsistent with the principle of restitution in kind or with that full restitution.[646] The negative attitude towards punitive damages is grounded on the policy consideration that Latvian civil law links civil liability with the compensatory function.[647] Likewise, another explanation refers to the very concept of the term 'damages' which covers a diminution

---

642. Specific injunctions are available in special cases such as infringments of intellectual property (Art. 250.[17] CPL).
643. Article 197(2) CPL.
644. Article 137(1) CPL.
645. Article 138(1)(5) CPL.
646. DCFR, *supra* n. 66, p. 3561.
647. *See* Ch. 4 of General Introduction of this monograph *supra*.

of property caused by an infringement of lawful civil law interests.[648] In this regard, an opinion is expressed in Latvian civil law literature that the difference theory (*Differenztheorie*) recognized in German and Swiss civil law may be exploited to explain diminution of property being at the heart of the concept of damages.[649] The difference theory may perhaps be recognized in Latvian court practice, though it does not use such a term.[650] Availability of punitive damages is also not accepted by Latvian civil-law scholars, who traditionally deny the punitive function of tort law.[651]

*374*. At the same time, despite the considerations discussed in the preceding paragraph, special legal provisions scattered among different legal acts demonstrate that Latvian civil law does actually admit punitive damages in certain cases.

*375*. The Civil Law does not enable a claimant to seek punitive damages in the case of a tort. For comparison, the Civil Law enables a claim for punitive damages in the case of contract law, yet only indirectly. Indeed, in the case of the *earnest money* obligation, a contract party who has not fulfilled the contract due to their fault is liable under that obligation in the amount of the earnest money.[652] In this situation, the duty to be liable in the amount of earnest money may be perceived as a meaning of a duty to cover punitive damages. This conclusion is attested to by the consideration that the law does not even provide possibility to review the amount payable either based on the degree of fault (ordinary or gross negligence) or the amount of damages actually suffered because damages (of a compensatory character) may be claimed in addition.[653]

*376*. Likewise, punitive damages are awarded in cases when damage is caused to *nature* on the basis of other legal acts. Latvian law provides that if a restricted hunting animal has been illegally hunted outside the hunting season specified in legal acts, the loss for each animal must be compensated twofold.[654] However, if a restricted hunting animal is injured in illegal hunting, the loss for each animal must be compensated in the amount of 50%.[655] Likewise, if creatures of specially protected species are destroyed or damaged in certain protected areas, the loss must be reimbursed threefold.[656] In addition, in the case of deforestation for which no

648. This idea is clearly based on the legal definition of the concept 'damages' included in Art. 1770 of the Civil Law.
649. Kalniņš, E. (2017), *supra* n. 529, 54–61.lpp.
650. Torgāns, K.; Kārkliņš, J.; Bitāns, A. (2017), *supra* n. 70, 271.lpp.
651. *See* Ch. 4 of the General Introduction of this monograph *supra*.
652. Article 1730(2) first sentence CL.
653. Article 1730(2) second sentence CL.
654. Regulatory enactment of the Cabinet No. 1482 'Rules for Compensation for Losses Caused by Violations of Legal Acts Regulating Hunting and the Value of Illegally Obtained Hunting Products' of 17 Dec. 2013, Point 5. No translation available.
655. *Ibid*, Point 6.
656. Regulatory enactment of the Cabinet No. 281 'Regulations Regarding Preventative and Rehabilitation Measures and the Procedures for Evaluation of Environmental Damage and Calculation of Costs of Preventative, Emergency and Rehabilitation Measures' of 24 Apr. 2007, Point 39. Official

compensation has been paid (with certain exceptions), the State Forest Service can recover triple compensation from the forest owner or legal possessor.[657]

*377.* The concept of punitive damages should *not* be *confused* with *presumption* of a certain amount of damages. Indeed, as we have seen (paragraphs 237 and 250 *supra*) the Competition Law envisages a presumption in cartel cases that the infringement has caused damage resulting in a price rise of 10%, unless proved otherwise.[658]

translation into English available on the official web-page of the State Language Centre at https://vvc.gov.lv/image/catalog/dokumenti/Cab._Reg._No._281_-_Regulations_Regarding_Preventative_and_Rehab.doc.

657. Point 19 Regulations on Criteria for Determining Deforestation Compensation, Calculation and Reimbursement Procedures [Noteikumi par atmežošanas kompensācijas noteikšanas kritērijiem, aprēķināšanas un atlīdzināšanas kārtību]. No 889, adopted on 18 Dec. 2012, entered into force on 1 Jan. 2013. Herald, No, 201, 21.12.2012.

658. Article 21(3) Competition Law.

# Selected Bibliography

Note that bibliography sources contain only sources on Latvian tort law published in English.


Damane L., Kārkliņš J., Lībiņa-Egner I., Mantrovs V., Ose D., Osis M., Rozenfelds J., Torgāns K., Zīle K. Private law, in: Kerikmäe T., Joamets K., Pleps J., Rodiņa A., Berkmanas T., Gruodytė E. (eds.). *The Law of the Baltic States*. Cham: Springer, 2017.

Karklins J. Main Modernization Directions of the Latvian Contract Law. *Summary of a doctoral thesis for the acquisition of a Doctor's degree in Jurisprudence*. Riga: University of Latvia, 2006.

Kārkliņš J. *Idea of Strict Liability in Private Law*. Journal of University of Latvia 'Law', 2017, No 10, pp. 175–199. Available also at https://www.journaloftheuniversityoflatvialaw.lu.lv/fileadmin/user_upload/lu_portal/projekti/journaloftheuniversityoflatvialaw/No10/J.Karklins.pdf.

Karklins, J. Third-parties as an Exclusion from Strict Liability, in: Legal Science: *Functions, Significance and Future in Legal Systems*, 16–18 October 2019, Riga: Collection of research papers in conjunction with the 7th International Scientific Conference of the Faculty of Law of the University of Latvia. Riga: University of Latvia Press, 2020, pp. 376–382. Available also at https://www.apgads.lu.lv/fileadmin/user_upload/lu_portal/apgads/PDF/Juridiskas-konferences/ISCFLUL-7-2019/Book-iscflul.7.2_.pdf.

Mantrov V. *Insurance Law in Latvia*. Kluwer Law International, 2018.

Schwartz P. Das Lettländische Zivilgezetzbuch vom 28. Januar 1937 und seine Entstehungsgeschichte. Aachen: Shaker Verlag, 2008.

Schwartz P. Lettland: Das Lettländische Zivilgesetzbuch vom 28. Januar 1937, in: Löhnig M., Wagner S. (Hrsg.) 'Nichtgeborene Kinder des Liberalismus?', Tübingen: Mohr Siebeck, 2018, S.317–358.

Torgāns K. Civiltiesību, komerctiesību un civilprocesa aktualitātes: raksti, 1999–2008. Current topics on civil, commercial law and civil procedure: selected articles, 1999–2008. Rīga: Tiesu namu aģentūra, 2009.

Torgāns K. *European Initiatives (PECL, DCFR) and Modernization of Latvian Civil Law*. Juridica International, 2008, No 14.

Torgāns K. Non-pecuniary (Moral) Damage in the Theory of Civil Law and Practice, in: *Jurisprudence and Culture: Past Lessons and Future Challenges*: the 5th International Scientific Conference of the University of Latvia dedicated to the 95th anniversary of the Faculty of Law of the University of Latvia, 10–11

November. Riga: University of Latvia Press, 2014, 600–621.lpp. Available also electronically at https://www.apgads.lu.lv/izdevumi/brivpieejas-izdevumi/rakstu-krajumi/.

Torgāns K. Fair *Judgment in Civil Cases as a Manifestation of Implementing Norms of the Satversme*, in: 6th International Conference 'Constitutional Values in Contemporary Legal Space II', 16–17 November, Riga, Latvia: Collection of Research Papers/Faculty of Law of the University of Latvia. Riga: University of Latvia, 2017, pp. 140–155. Available also electronically at https://dspace.lu.lv/dspace/handle/7/37224.

Torgāns K. Latvian civil law and the draft of the European contract code. A l' Europe du troisieme millenaire: melanges offerts a (essays in honour of, Festschrift fur, homenaje a, studi in onore di) Giuseppe Gandolfi a l'occasion du dixieme anniversaire de la fondation de l'Academie/Academie desprivatistes europeens = Academy of European private lawyers. Vol. 4. Milano: A. Giuffre, 2009, pp. 1829–1845.

Torgāns K. *Essential cases on natural causation*: Latvia, in: Winiger B., Koziol H. [et al.] (eds.) Digest of European tort law. Vol. 1. Wien, NewYork: Springer, 2007.

Torgāns K. *Essential cases on damage*: Latvia, in: Koziol H. [et al.] (eds.). Digest of European tort law. Vol. 2. Berlin: De Gruyter, 2011.

Torgāns K., Kubilis J. *Essential cases on misconduct*: Latvia, in: Winiger B. [et al.] (eds). Digest of European tort law. Vol. 3. De Gruyter, 2018.

Torgāns K., Kārkliņš J., Mantrov V., Rasnačs L. *Contract Law in Latvia*. AH Alphen aan den Rijn: Kluwer, 2020.

# Index

*The numbers here refer to paragraph numbers.*

## Index

www.ingramcontent.com/pod-product-compliance
Lightning Source LLC
Chambersburg PA
CBHW071344230926
51846CB00002B/443
* 9 7 8 9 4 0 3 5 2 3 8 6 6 *